Magical Metal Clay Jewellery

Amazingly simple no-kiln
techniques for making
beautiful jewellery

Sue Heaser

D&C
David and Charles

www.mycraftivity.com
CONNECT. CREATE. EXPLORE.

A DAVID & CHARLES BOOK

David & Charles is an
F+W Publications Inc. company
4700 East Galbraith Road
Cincinnati, OH 45236

Conceived, designed and produced by
Quarto Publishing plc
The Old Brewery
6 Blundell Street
London N7 9BH

ISBN-13: 978-0-7153-2765-4 paperback
ISBN-10: 0-7153-2765-8 paperback

Colour separation by SC (Sang Choy)
International Pte Ltd, Singapore

Printed in China by SNP Leefung Printers Ltd
for David & Charles
Brunel House   Newton Abbot   Debon

For Quarto Publishing plc
Editor: Michelle Pickering
Proofreader: Julia Halford
Indexer: Dorothy Frame
Art director: Caroline Guest
Managing art editor: Anna Plucinska
Designer: Elizabeth Healey
Photographer: Phil Wilkins
Illustrator: Kuo Kang Chen
Picture researcher: Sarah Bell
Creative director: Moira Clinch
Publisher: Paul Carslake

QUA: MCJ

Visit our website at www.davidandcharles.co.uk

David & Charles books are available from all
good bookshops; alternatively you can contact
our Orderline on 0870 9908222 or write to us
at FREEPOST EX2 110, D&C Direct, Newton
Abbot, TQ12 4ZZ (no stamp required UK only);
US customers call 800-289-0963 and
Canadian customers call 800-840-5220.

Contents

Introduction

Metal clay is a relatively recent invention in the world of art and craft. Its description often produces disbelief from the listener – people find it astonishing that firing a little grey piece of clay with a blowtorch will turn it into pure silver or gold. But yes, it is true, even though it appears to be a modern form of alchemy.

Metal clay is made from powdered precious metal combined with an organic binder and water. It can be modelled, moulded or sculpted in a way similar to ceramic clay or polymer clay. When heated to a high temperature, the binder burns away and the precious metal particles sinter (or fuse) into solid silver or gold.

The history of metal clay as an art and craft material is surprisingly short. It was invented in Japan in the early 1990s, and since then has taken the jewellery and craft worlds by storm. It is available all over the world, and a rapidly growing body of artists is embracing its extraordinary capabilities.

Two main brands are available: Precious Metal Clay (PMC) made by Mitsubishi Materials Corporation, and Art Clay manufactured by Aida Chemical Industries Co Ltd. Each company produces a variety of different kinds of metal clay. New and improved versions have appeared regularly over the past ten years. While each brand has a different patent, the techniques used for them are virtually identical.

In the past few years, both manufacturers have introduced types of silver metal clay that can be fired at a lower temperature than the earlier versions, using a small blowtorch or a gas hob in the kitchen. This exciting development has made the clays accessible to the home hobbyist or casual user – there is no need for expensive tools or a kiln.

This book is aimed at just such a user, and all the projects in the main part of the book can be fired using silver metal clay and these simple methods. Kiln owners are not forgotten, however, with a final chapter that includes projects using delicious dichroic glass as well as the fragile and beautiful paper or sheet clay.

If you are a beginner, you are about to discover the fabulous qualities of this magical substance that turns into pure silver before your eyes. If you are more experienced in metal clays, then I hope you will find many new discoveries in this book.

Materials

The new generation of low-fire metal clays are easy for the home crafter to use, and the projects in the book are all made with these. The main types are listed here. There are also many other exciting materials that you can use to embellish and enhance your metal clay jewellery.

Art Clay 650

Art Clay 650 Slow Dry

PMC+

PMC3

METAL CLAY

SILVER CLAY – LUMP FORM

The standard type of metal clay comes in the form of a lump, just like ceramic clay or polymer clay. This is the type of clay required whenever a project simply lists 'silver metal clay'. Projects that require more time to work specify slow-dry silver metal clay, because it gives about four times the working time before it begins to dry out. It is also an ideal choice for beginners. If slow-dry clay is not specified, then any of the four types of lump clay listed below can be used. All of the clays come in various package sizes, from 5g through to 100g. If you are a beginner, stick to projects that use 10g of clay or less. See page 20 for advice on storing metal clay.

SILVER CLAY PASTE OR SLIP

This paste or slip form of metal clay has many uses, from attaching findings to painting fine layers of silver. You can make your own by adding water to the lump form of the clay, or purchase the ready-made variety. These clays have similar properties to their lump clay counterparts.

- Art Clay 650 Paste Type
- PMC+ or PMC3 Slip

SILVER CLAY SYRINGE

Metal clay paste is also available in a ready-filled syringe. You can use different-sized nozzles (or cut down a fine one) for piping lines of filigree.

- Art Clay 650 Syringe Type
- PMC+ or PMC3 Syringe Type

SILVER PAPER OR SHEET CLAY

This type of clay uses papercraft techniques, including cutting, folding and quilling. The Art Clay brand feels like thick paper and holds its shape well when folded or creased. The PMC brand is thinner and feels more like fine leather. Both types are kiln-fire only.

- Art Clay Paper Type
- PMC+ Sheet

ART CLAY SILVER OIL PASTE

This is a wonderful product if you have a kiln (it is kiln-fire only). Use it to attach findings to fired silver, and to mend silver pieces that have broken.

GOLD METAL CLAY

Gold metal clay is available in both Art Clay and PMC, but can only be fired in a kiln and is very expensive. It is only available in lump form or as an embellishing paste. The modelling techniques are the same as those described for silver clay, but you will need to refer to the manufacturer's instructions for specific firing guidelines.

ART CLAY 650
- Low-fire clay
- Shrinkage: 8–10%
- Firing: Gas burner, blowtorch or kiln

PMC+
- Medium- to low-fire clay
- Shrinkage: 10–15%
- Firing: Blowtorch or kiln – not recommended for gas burner

ART CLAY 650 SLOW DRY
- Low-fire clay
- Shrinkage: 8–10%
- Firing: Gas burner, blowtorch or kiln

PMC3
- Low-fire clay
- Shrinkage: 10–15%
- Firing: Gas burner, blowtorch or kiln

Clay syringe

Oil paste

Clay paste or slip

Paper clay

Sheet clay

Gold paste

Gold leaf

Gemstones

Polymer clay

OTHER MATERIALS

GOLD PASTE

Pure gold in a liquid form, this product can be used to add pure gold accents to fired silver clay. There are several brands available; application methods are similar, but check the instructions on the package.
- Art Clay Gold Paste
- Aura 22 Gold Paste by PMC
- Accent Gold for Silver

GOLD LEAF

This is used to apply pure gold accents to fired silver. Use thick gold leaf available from metal clay suppliers and enamellers.

LIVER OF SULPHUR

This oxidizing material is used to antique or colour the silver. It comes in both lump and solution form. Store it sealed and away from light or it will deteriorate.

RESIN

Two-part epoxy resin is used to simulate enamelling or as a protective coating over mother-of-pearl mosaic. Use an epoxy resin that is a coating epoxy rather than an embedding epoxy, because it is thicker and easier to control. Brand names include Envirotex Lite, Crystal Sheen, Solid Water and Colores Cold Enamels. Use oil paints to colour the resin, or the colours supplied by the manufacturer. UV resin is an alternative kind that is hardened using exposure to UV light. It requires a UV light cabinet, which is available from some metal clay suppliers.

POLYMER CLAY

With its wide range of colours, polymer clay combines beautifully with metal clay. Use a strong clay, such as Fimo, Premo Sculpey or Kato Clay.

FINDINGS

Findings are the metal pieces that are attached to your silver creations to make them into wearable jewellery. Pure silver findings can be fired with the clay and are the best to use for embedding. Sterling silver findings are more widely available, but will blacken and become brittle if fired for too long on a gas burner or with a blowtorch. They can be safely fired at the lower firing temperatures in a kiln. When findings can be added after firing, such as chains and jump rings, sterling silver is a good choice because it is stronger than pure silver.

WIRE

Use pure silver wire for embedding and firing with the clay, and sterling silver wire for other wire requirements. Wire that is 0.6–0.8mm is a good all-purpose size.

GEMSTONES

Manmade gemstones, such as cubic zirconia, can be fired with metal clay by blowtorch or on a gas burner, provided they are 5mm diameter or less. They come in a sumptuous array of colours and shapes. Check that the gems can be fired before you buy.

DICHROIC GLASS

This glorious coloured glass is available in a huge variety of colours and patterns. Be sure always to use glass of the same COE (coefficient of expansion), such as COE 90. It is available from glass fusing specialists. The thinner kinds (1.5–2mm) are best for making small jewellery cabochons.

Dichroic glass

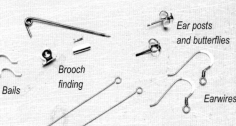

Ear posts and butterflies

Brooch finding

Bails

Earwires

Screw eyes

Eyepins

Jump rings

Headpins

Bezels

Resin

Liver of sulphur

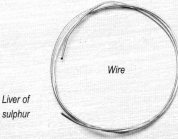

Wire

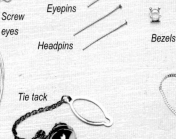

Tie tack

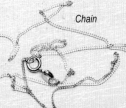

Chain

Equipment

The basic tools needed for working with metal clay are relatively simple, inexpensive and accessible. The main tools used to make the projects in this book are described here; some projects require extra tools, and these are listed with the project.

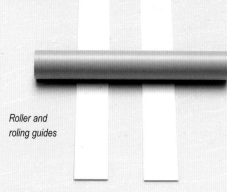

Roller and roling guides

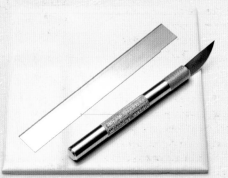

Ceramic tile with tissue blade and craft knife

BASIC TOOLKIT

Certain tools are required for the majority of the projects. To avoid repetition, the projects specify a basic toolkit that should contain:
• Suitable work surface
• Ceramic tiles (two or three would be useful, but one will often do)
• Craft knife
• Roller and rolling guides
• Blunt and sharp needles or needle tools
• Water pot
• Paintbrushes
• Cling film
• Ruler
• Drying equipment
• Firing equipment and tweezers for quenching (cooling)

FOR SOFT CLAY

WORK SURFACE
• Smooth, washable surface: This is essential when working with wet clay. A sheet of glass with the edges sanded is ideal, because it can be placed over graph paper to give guidelines. You can improvise with a melamine tablemat or Formica tabletop.
• Ceramic tile: This is invaluable as a movable work surface. You can work wet on the tile and then place the tile in the oven to dry the piece without moving it. Small 10cm square white or cream tiles with a smooth glaze are ideal.
• Non-stick rolling surface: Plastic file wallets (from stationers) that have a slight texture make excellent non-stick rolling surfaces. Baking parchment is slightly absorbent, so it is best used only when the clay is too wet.

CUTTING TOOLS
• Craft knife: Use a knife with a curved blade; you will find that it is far more versatile than a straight blade.
• Tissue blades: These long, straight blades are used to cut straight lines on clay sheets to make strips, squares and rectangles.

ROLLING TOOLS
Sheets of clay are one of the basic requirements of working in metal clay, and the basis for many projects.
• Roller: Simple plastic tube rollers are the best to use for metal clay and are widely available. You can improvise with a small bottle. A sheet of Perspex is useful for rolling smooth, even logs, especially long, thin logs.
• Rolling guides: Pairs of acrylic strips in different thicknesses are available from metal clay suppliers. Two stacks of playing cards are a useful alternative; you can vary the number of cards to achieve different clay sheet thicknesses.

PIERCING TOOLS
• Tapestry or wool needle: A thick, blunt 3mm thick needle is a very useful tool for making holes and smoothing clay.
• Darning needle: Use this thinner, sharper needle for making holes.
• Needle tool: A needle mounted in a wooden handle can be more comfortable to use.

PAINTBRUSHES
Use artists' paintbrushes for applying paste and for brushing the clay with water to moisten it. Round artificial-fibre brushes are best – size 1 to 3 for paste and water; smaller sizes (0 or 00) for applying gold paste.

Needle tool with sharp po...

Blunt tapestry needle

Paintbrush

Sculpting tools

Cocktail sticks

Brush protectors

Rubber stamps

Rubber texture sheet

Heat gun

Mesh

Mandrel

Cutters

Ring gauge and sticky notes

SCULPTING AND SHAPING TOOLS

- Tapestry or wool needle: This piercing tool is also perfect for miniature sculpting, and the stainless steel surface is ideal for working wet clay.
- Dental tools and small sculpting tools: These come in a range of shapes and are available from sculpting suppliers. Use a ball-ended tool for sculpting; use a tool with a spatula shape for applying paste and smoothing.
- Cocktail sticks: These are useful as needles, for stirring paste and for wrapping strips of clay around to make bails.
- Brush protectors: These are the small, clear tubes that protect the ends of artists' paintbrushes. Use them for cutting out holes in clay, texturing and as a core for wrapping a strip of clay to make a loop. A drinking straw can be used instead.

CUTTERS

There are many different ready-made cutters available. Choose open-ended cutters in small sizes. Good-quality cutters with butt-soldered joins are best, because they will not make unwelcome dents in the edges of a clay shape.

STAMPS AND TEXTURE SHEETS

The rapidly growing craft of polymer clay has provided the clay artist with a wonderful selection of rubber stamps and texture sheets. Choose those with clear lines, high relief and detailed designs.

RING-MAKING TOOLS

- Mandrel: This round stick tapers along its length so that you can wrap clay around different points on the stick to create different ring sizes.
- Ring gauge: A simple card ring gauge is adequate for measuring ring sizes, but a metal or plastic gauge is easier to use accurately.
- Sticky notes: Use these to cover the mandrel to prevent the clay from sticking to it. Proprietary sheets with a ring gauge can be used, or cut your own from a sticky note.

DRYING EQUIPMENT

- Oven: A home oven is the best way of drying metal clay thoroughly. Use a simple metal baking pan to hold the pieces when placing them in the oven. Tiles with work on them can be placed directly on the oven shelves.
- Hair drier: Use a hair drier for partially drying metal clay to give it enough strength before placing it in the oven to dry fully.
- Heat gun: An alternative to a hair drier, a heat gun used for embossing powders is much hotter and will dry clay rapidly.
- Mesh: Place metal clay pieces onto a stainless steel mesh when drying with a hair drier or heat gun. This is the same mesh used for gas burner firing.

FOR DRIED AND FIRED CLAY

FILES

A fine half-round needle file is the most useful kind for smoothing rough edges and for carving decorations. Large hand files, both medium and fine, are useful for smoothing larger areas. Clean files by brushing along their teeth with a stainless steel brush.

Fine half-round needle file

Large hand file

Sanding pads

Sandpaper

Engraving tool

SANDING MATERIALS

Plaster-dry metal clay can be sanded very easily to a smooth surface. This is usually necessary to remove filing marks or fingerprints left from the wet stage.

- Sanding pads: These are ideal for metal clay. They are composed of a sanding surface backed by a thin layer of sponge, so they curve around any shape with ease as you sand. When clogged with plaster-dry clay, they can be washed to prolong their life. Cut the pads into small pieces for handier sizes – about 2.5 x 5cm. Use the coarser grit for sanding dry clay, and all three in succession from coarse to fine for creating a mirror finish on fired silver. The three grits are:
Superfine: 320–600 grit (coarse)
Ultrafine: 800–1000 grit (medium)
Microfine: 1200–1500 grit (fine)
- Sandpaper: This can be used as an alternative to sanding pads; use similar grades as above. Sandpaper is useful for sanding the sides of rings and other straight edges.

ENGRAVING TOOLS

Plaster-dry metal clay is easy to engrave. Use any tool with a point, such as a burnisher or a clutch pencil engraver.

DRILLING TOOLS

It is easiest to drill holes in metal clay at the plaster-dry stage, but these tools can be used on solid silver as well.

- Pin vice: This small handheld tool will take different-sized drill bits.
- Drill bits: These can be used on their own for plaster-dry clay, but will need a pin vice for solid silver. Useful sizes are 1mm, 1.5mm and 2mm.

RUBBER BLOCK

A solid block of hard rubber is an excellent surface for working on plaster-dry and fired metal clay. The rubber will not damage the piece, and prevents it from sliding as you file, drill or sand.

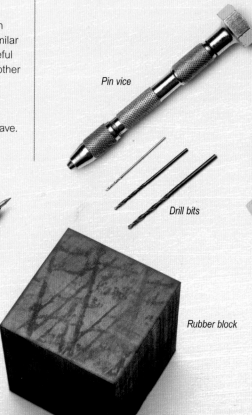

Pin vice

Drill bits

Rubber block

BRUSHES

Use these to brush over the silver surface after firing to remove the white frosty fired surface and begin the polishing process.

- Stainless steel brushes: A long-bristled brush is used for most projects, allowing you to reach into recesses and corners. A short-bristled brush is needed to reach inside a ring shank. A fine brush is available for brushing tiny crevices and hard-to-reach areas.
- Fibreglass brushes: These are a gentler version of the stainless steel brushes and usually come as clutch pencils of different sizes.

TWEEZERS

These are used to hold hot pieces when quenching (cooling) the fired silver, and also for holding silver when oxidizing.

BURNISHERS

Use burnishers to shine areas of silver that are textured, or edges of pieces where sanding is difficult. Do not use them for larger flat areas – they will always leave lines.

- Stainless steel burnisher: This is available in various sizes; smaller is better for small jewellery pieces.
- Agate burnisher: Use a burnisher with an agate tip for shining applied gold leaf and paste.

POLISH

Silver polish and a soft cloth add the final shine at the end of all your hard work. Ordinary household silver polish works beautifully on the bright pure silver of metal clay. You can use a proprietary polishing cloth (some are impregnated with polish) or rags from an old T-shirt.

WIRE CUTTERS AND PLIERS

You will need a pair of wire cutters and some fine pliers (ideally round nose) for cutting and bending wire and attaching findings.

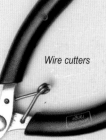
Wire cutters

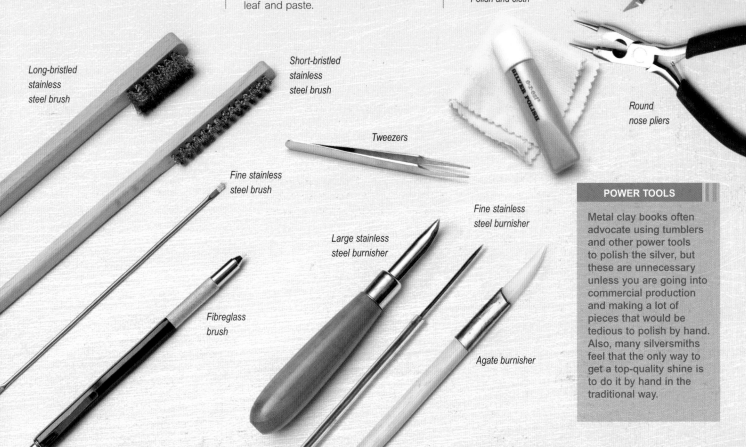

Long-bristled stainless steel brush

Short-bristled stainless steel brush

Fine stainless steel brush

Fibreglass brush

Tweezers

Large stainless steel burnisher

Fine stainless steel burnisher

Agate burnisher

Polish and cloth

Round nose pliers

POWER TOOLS

Metal clay books often advocate using tumblers and other power tools to polish the silver, but these are unnecessary unless you are going into commercial production and making a lot of pieces that would be tedious to polish by hand. Also, many silversmiths feel that the only way to get a top-quality shine is to do it by hand in the traditional way.

FOR GAS BURNER FIRING

Easy for beginners to master, gas burner firing is an efficient way of firing silver clay – several pieces can be fired at a time on the mesh. There are many different types of gas burners and stoves available, and most are excellent for firing metal clay.

Single-burner camping gas stove

GAS BURNER

- Domestic gas hob: Gas is used for domestic cooking in many parts of the world, and if your kitchen has this kind of burner, you have your firing equipment already at hand. Use the hottest burner on full heat.
- Camping gas stove: A camping gas stove is excellent for firing metal clay, because these stoves usually have a hot flame and they are often less expensive than a good blowtorch.

There are many different types of stove available, as well as different types of fuel. A single-burner camping gas stove that uses either butane or propane in a bottle is inexpensive and widely available all over the world.

STAINLESS STEEL MESH OR NET
You will need a mesh at least 10 x 15cm to cover the burner of the stove.

Stainless steel mesh

FOR BLOWTORCH FIRING

Firing with the intense flame of a blowtorch is the quickest method of all, but care must be taken not to melt the silver.

Blowtorch

BLOWTORCH
The most widely used for metal clay is a handheld refillable blowtorch that uses canisters of butane gas available from supermarkets. A blowtorch that has an adjustable air/gas mixture is the best kind, because you can use a medium-hot flame for firing and this is less likely to melt the silver.

FIRE BRICK OR FIBRE BRICK
Fire bricks of the fibre type are lightweight, but you can use any kind of firing brick sold for use with blowtorches.

Fire brick

FOR KILN FIRING

As you become more skilled with metal clay, you may feel it worthwhile to buy a small kiln for firing glass and paper clay, and for other more advanced techniques. A kiln is also a good investment if you plan to go into production jewellery.

KILN

A small jewellery kiln with a firing chamber about 15cm across or smaller is ideal. It should have a built-in pyrometer (a thermometer that measures the very high temperatures in a kiln) and a controller (to keep the temperature at the correct level).

KILN FURNITURE

This is the term used for the heatproof boards and props that you use in the kiln to support the silver while firing.

- Firing board or kiln shelf: Lightweight fibre firing boards are the easiest to use, and can be cut to size as required.
- Props: Small kiln props are available to support the firing board above the kiln floor, but you can improvise by using cut-up pieces of firing board as props.
- Fibre cloth: This heatproof cloth or blanket is used to support small pieces of silver on the firing board.

OTHER KILN EQUIPMENT

- Ceramic paper or firing paper: Use this to cover a kiln shelf when firing glass to prevent the glass from sticking to the shelf.
- Tongs: You will need a simple pair of kitchen tongs to remove hot firing board from the kiln.
- Gloves and goggles: Heatproof gloves and kiln goggles are optional extras to protect you from the kiln heat.

TIP

Always fire new firing board and fibre cloth before use at about 500ºC for a few minutes to remove any impurities that might affect the silver.

Firing board

Fibre cloth

Small jewellery kiln

Tongs

Ceramic paper

Basic Techniques

Metal clay goes through three different stages while it is being worked: soft clay, plaster-dry clay and pure silver. This chapter describes the basic techniques for working on each of the three stages in detail, as well as providing instructions for drying and firing the clay.

Getting started

Keeping the clay in a perfect state of moistness is the key to success when working with metal clay. Before you begin your first project, it is a good idea to have a trial run to familiarize yourself with metal clay, and get comfortable working with it and remoistening it.

WORKING WITH METAL CLAY

STEP 1
Take the clay out of the package. Keep the resealable outer package handy for storing unused clay (see Storing Metal Clay on page 20). The inner pack varies between brands – some have a sealed pocket, others just a piece of cling film.

STEP 2
Clay is usually in perfect condition when it comes out of the pack, but it is best to knead it with your fingers for a moment or two to make sure that the moisture is well distributed through the clay.

STEP 3
Now try rolling the clay into a sheet, making some small balls, and generally familiarizing yourself with the clay. If you are using slow-dry clay, you will be able to work for a while before it shows any signs of drying or cracking. If you are using any other type of metal clay, the room is hot or you have very hot hands, it will dry more quickly.

STEP 4
If the clay still feels soft, wrap it in a piece of cling film and tuck it back in the resealable pack, or place it in a small sealable plastic pot. If it has dry areas developing, remoisten it before storing.

TIPS
- If you are a beginner, use a slow-dry clay to give yourself more time.
- Use a small pack of clay for your first experiments – a 7–10g pack is ideal for first projects.
- Get all your tools ready before you open the clay pack, so that the clay does not start to dry out while you gather things.
- Cover the clay with cling film to prevent it from drying when you need a break, and keep a small pot of water nearby for remoistening the clay.
- Use a piece of polymer clay for a dummy run of any project. Because it will not dry out in your hands like metal clay, it will give you valuable thinking and designing time – especially useful for beginners.

MOISTENING THE CLAY

When the clay becomes too dry, cracks will appear at the edges and on the surface. This means you need to add water. The trick is to add water to the inside of the clay lump, not the surface.

STEP 1
Roll out the clay as thinly as possible on a non-stick surface. This will also crush any dry lumps within the clay.

STEP 2
Apply water with a fingertip all over the surface. Do not flood the clay; just apply a thin film of water.

STEP 3
Fold the clay sheet in half with the water inside. Fold again and place the clay in a piece of cling film to knead it.

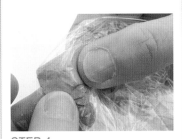

STEP 4
Squeeze the clay firmly inside the cling film to make a bigger pancake. Open up the film, fold again and repeat a few times. Now take it out of the film and knead it in your fingers to check that it is soft and smooth. Repeat the moistening process if necessary. If you make the clay too wet, roll it out inside a folded sheet of baking parchment to absorb the excess moisture.

too dry   just right   too wet

RECONSTITUTING DRY CLAY

Metal clay can be rehydrated and reused repeatedly until it is fired. Clay that has been allowed to dry into a rock-hard state can either be used to make paste (see Making Paste on page 25), or reconstituted into a moist and malleable state.

STEP 1
Make a cut in the centre of a sponge at least 2.5cm deep. Wet the sponge and then squeeze it out so that it is still moist but does not drip. Push the clay lump well into the slit in the sponge and place the sponge in a bowl with a little water in the bottom.

TIPS

- If you also work with ceramic clay, you may be tempted to keep the clay surface wet all the time, but this is wasteful when working with metal clay because you are working with such small quantities.
- The slip that builds up on your hands when working with overly wet metal clay makes the clay hard to control. Working metal clay with the surface touch-dry gives far more control.
- There is no need to oil your hands, as is sometimes recommended. Oil should only be used when impressing the clay with textures or stamps; for all other purposes, it is best avoided, because it prevents the clay from sticking well to itself when pieces are added.

STEP 2
Cover the bowl with cling film. Leave for several hours or overnight, then remove the clay from the sponge and knead it in a piece of cling film. The wetness will depend on the ambient temperature and type of sponge, so you will need to experiment as to how long to leave the clay for it to rehydrate. If the clay is not wet enough, either leave it in the sponge for longer or remoisten the clay in the usual way if it is malleable but a bit too firm. If the clay is too wet, leave it unwrapped for a while to dry out a little. It is better to have it not wet enough than too wet.

Shaping soft clay

Many metal clay projects use a range of basic skills, such as rolling logs and forming balls. These are skills that most of us learned as children using modelling clay, and can easily be adapted to the smaller scale required for metal clay. You will learn additional shaping techniques as you work through the projects in the book.

ROLLING LOGS

Rolling an even log in metal clay can be done by hand or with a sheet of Perspex.

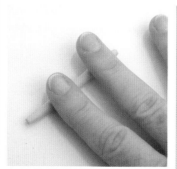

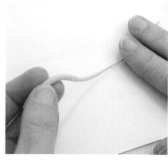

STEP 1

To roll by hand, shape the clay into a ball and then roll the ball between your hands to start shaping the log. Place the clay on a non-stick surface and roll it back and forth with your fingers, keeping the fingers moving constantly along the length of the log to keep it an even thickness.

STEP 2

For a more even log, and to prevent heat from your hands from drying the clay, use a small clear rigid sheet, such as a piece of Perspex or a CD case, to roll the clay back and forth. You will need to press quite firmly, but very even logs can be made in this way.

STEP 3

For extra-thin threads of clay, roll a log in the usual way and then hold one end in one hand. Use the other hand to roll the clay into a thin thread, pulling it outwards from the thicker part as you work. The thicker part can be used as a handle to control the clay thread when coiling or curving it onto a clay surface. Slow-dry clay is ideal for making very thin threads, because they can dry out quickly.

FORMING BALLS AND TEARDROPS

Small balls of clay are used in many ways, such as for embellishments and tiny beads. Teardrops are another pretty and useful shape.

 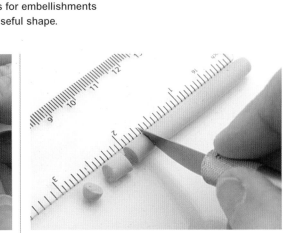 

STEP 1

Pinch off a piece of clay of the size required and lay it on the first two fingers of one hand. Cover it with the same two fingers of the other hand and rotate these in a circular motion to make a little ball.

STEP 2

To make balls of equal size, roll a log first and place it alongside a ruler. Cut equal lengths to roll into balls.

STEP 3

To shape a teardrop, roll one side of the ball between your fingers to make a point.

ROLLING SHEETS

Sheets are the starting point of many different projects. Use rolling guides – acrylic strips or playing cards – to make sure that the clay sheet is rolled to an even thickness all over.

STEP 1

Flatten the clay into a small pancake and lay it on a non-stick surface between rolling guides of the required thickness. Roll over the surface of the clay, turning it 90 degrees halfway through. Take care not to stretch the clay as you roll or it may shrink irregularly during firing.

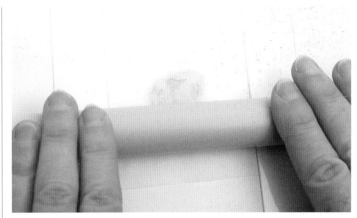

STEP 2

If the clay is sticky, place it between two sheets of baking parchment to roll it out.

Drying the clay

When you have finished working the clay in the soft stage, it is time to dry it. There are various ways of drying metal clay, and this differs between brands and clay types. I recommend using an oven. It is easy to dry clay in this way, and you can be sure that it is completely dry if you follow the guidelines below.

DOMESTIC OVEN

This simple method can be used for all kinds of metal clay, including slow-dry clay. A fan oven is the best kind, because it circulates air as well. Place the clay on a ceramic tile or baking sheet and put into an oven set to 150ºC for 30 minutes. All pieces that are 6mm thick or less will be bone dry in this time. If the piece is thicker, you should leave it for longer. Slow-dry clay should be dried in the same way, but at 180ºC.

HOTPLATE AND MUG WARMERS

An electric hotplate set to a low setting will dry metal clay successfully. Mug warmers can also be used. You will need to experiment to check how long to leave a piece to dry with an appliance, because they vary so much.

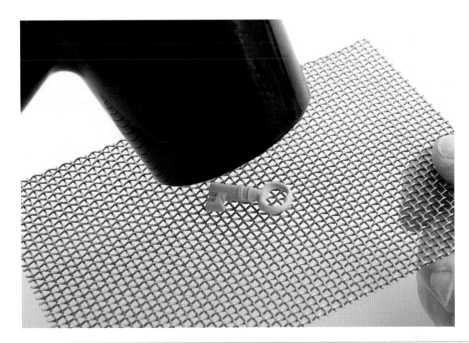

HAIR DRIER

An ordinary hair drier is useful for drying metal clay after pasting, mending or adding findings. If you have added a lot of soft clay or paste, it is safer to use an oven. Place the piece to be dried on a mesh and hold the mesh by the edge and well above the work surface to allow the hot air to pass freely through the mesh. Switch on the hair drier and hold the end of the nozzle about 2.5–5cm from the piece, keeping the drier moving. The hot air will pass through the mesh all around the piece and prevent it from being blown away. You will need to continue for at least 2–3 minutes to dry surface pasting and added findings.

- Metal clay must be completely dried all the way through or it may split or crack during firing, like this moulded shell.
- You should always check the manufacturer's drying instructions on the pack of clay.
- You can dry pieces at room temperature or in a warm place overnight, but to be completely sure they are dry, it is safest to use added heat.

CRAFT EMBOSSING
HEAT GUN

Heat guns are used for papercraft embossing powder projects and are ideal for drying metal clay rapidly instead of using a hair drier. They have a much higher temperature than a hair drier and a gentler fan speed, so the piece is less likely to blow away. They are also much quieter. They operate at a temperature of around 360°C, so you must use the heat fairly sparingly or the binder in the metal clay may begin to burn off. Place the clay piece on a ceramic tile and apply the heat to dry small areas of added paste or soft clay. The clay will rapidly become too hot to touch, so take care; 10–15 seconds is usually sufficient for surface drying.

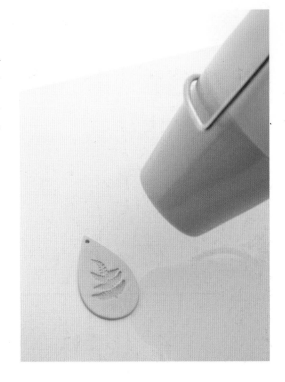

Pre-finishing techniques

Once the clay is completely dry, you can file, sand, drill or engrave it. Cracks, irregularities and broken pieces can also be mended with paste. Refining pieces at the plaster-dry stage will save a lot of hard work after firing when the clay has become solid silver, but take care because plaster-dry clay is fairly fragile.

FILING

If there are any major rough edges on the piece, file them away with a fine file. Take care because the plaster-dry clay will crack if you put too much pressure on it, and the file will bite through the clay very quickly. Support the piece well in your fingers as you file.

DRILLING

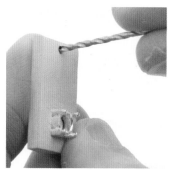

To make neat holes in metal clay pieces, make a small pilot hole with a needle while the clay is still soft, and then drill the hole with a fine drill bit when the clay is plaster-dry. You can simply twist the drill bit with your fingers to drill a hole in a thin piece. Too much pressure may crack the clay, so place a finger as a support behind the point where you are drilling. For holes in thicker pieces of dry clay, use a pin vice to hold the drill bit.

ENGRAVING

STEP 1

Engraving is a wonderful way to personalize your silverwork and is much easier to do in the plaster-dry state. Make sure that the piece is thick enough to take the engraving – at least 1mm thick. Start by drawing a design in pencil on the surface of the dried clay. If you make a mistake, simply sand the drawn lines away.

STEP 2

Use an engraving tool or even a pointed needle to inscribe the clay along the pencil lines. Support the clay from behind as you work to avoid breaking it with the pressure. It is best to mark the lines fairly lightly at first and then go over them repeatedly to deepen them. Brush away the excess clay with a paintbrush as you work.

SANDING

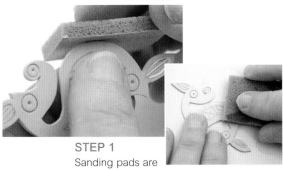

STEP 1

Sanding pads are best for sanding away rough areas on plaster-dry clay, because they bend around the piece. You can also sand over the surface of a piece to smooth it for a mirror finish. Use the coarsest grit (superfine 320–600 grit) for sanding at this stage.

STEP 2

Sandpaper is useful for sanding the sides of band rings to make sure that they are perfectly flat and smooth. Lay the sandpaper face up on the work surface and rub the ring, on its side, in a circular motion on the sandpaper.

MENDING WITH PASTE

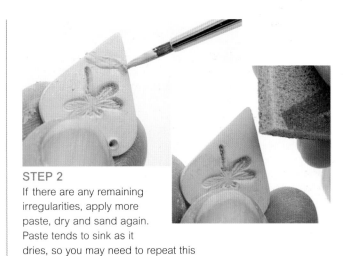

STEP 1

Apply paste liberally to one of the broken edges. Press the pieces together so that they are perfectly aligned; prop if necessary. Dry thoroughly, then sand or file away the excess clay.

STEP 2

If there are any remaining irregularities, apply more paste, dry and sand again. Paste tends to sink as it dries, so you may need to repeat this process until the area is smooth. After firing, the join should be invisible.

MAKING PASTE

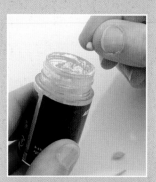

- Add small scraps of clay (soft or dried out) to a jar with a lid and cover with water. Leave overnight and then stir thoroughly. You can regularly add scraps to this jar, adding more water as necessary.
- If the paste is lumpy, scrape it out onto a tile and use a spatula to crush any lumps and refine the paste.
- You can use the waste clay from filing or engraving, but do not use the dust from sanding because it will be contaminated by the abrasive particles from the sandpaper.
- Avoid mixing different types of clay in one paste pot; they have different binders and may have different firing temperatures. Keep a paste pot for each type of clay you use.
- Apply paste with a paintbrush, cocktail stick or small spatula.

Firing the clay

There are three ways of firing metal clay: on a gas burner, with a blowtorch or with a kiln. The resulting fired pure silver should be equally successful with all methods, provided instructions are followed accurately. Gas burner and blowtorch firing can be used for all of the projects in this book, except for the kiln-fired projects in the final chapter.

FIRING TEST

It is important to fire metal clay properly, or it will not reach full strength. During firing, the binder first burns off with a small visible flame and small quantity of smoke; the piece then shrinks and appears to turn white. Finally, it glows a pale orange colour; it needs to be kept at this stage for the full specified time, which varies depending on the firing method. This last stage is called 'sintering', and involves the particles of silver being heated to just below melting point so that they form a solid mass. The result is a strong and durable silver, although not quite as strong as cast silver. If the clay is not fully sintered, it will be fragile and break easily. It is therefore wise to do a test firing to be sure that all is well with your chosen firing method.

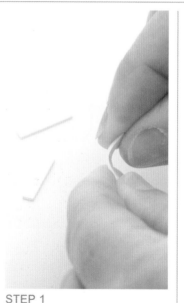

STEP 1
Roll out a sheet of clay, 1mm thick, and cut some 3 x 25mm strips from it. Dry and then fire the strips using one of the firing methods (see pages 27–29). Cool the strips and then try bending them in half.

STEP 2
You should be able to bend each piece into a complete U-bend without it snapping. If it breaks before this point, then the piece is not fully fired. Another indicator of inadequate firing is if the piece has not shrunk the full amount stated by the manufacturer, but this is difficult to test accurately with small pieces. Check the list of firing problems (see box), adjust your firing technique as necessary and perform another test.

GAS BURNER FIRING

This is the easiest way to fire metal clay, particularly if you have a gas hob in your kitchen for cooking. If you do not, then a single-burner camping gas stove is an excellent alternative. You will also need a stainless steel mesh to place on the burner. The dried metal clay piece is placed on the mesh, the gas burner is lit and the piece is fired for the required time. Art Clay Silver is recommended for this type of firing, but excellent results are achievable with low-fire PMC3 as well. Maximum recommended size is a piece of clay weighing 25g; the piece should fit entirely within a glowing red spot on the mesh.

STEP 1
Lay the stainless steel mesh on the burner and turn the flame on full to check the position of the hottest spots on the mesh. These will glow bright red.

STEP 2
Turn off the gas and place the dried clay piece on an area that glowed bright red. Make sure that the glowing area is big enough to heat all parts of the piece.

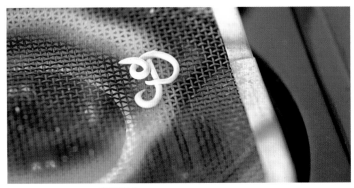

STEP 3
Turn on the burner again. After a few moments, the metal clay will give off a little smoke and flame, which is the binder burning away. This will go out of its own accord.

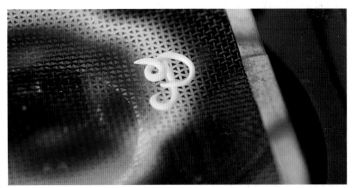

STEP 4
Continue firing until the clay glows a pale orange colour. This may be difficult to see in a bright room, so it is best to fire clay for the first time at night so that you can control the light levels in the room. Now time the firing for at least 5 minutes. When the time is up, switch off the burner and either allow the silver to cool or quench it (see page 29).

CHOOSING A SUITABLE FIRING METHOD

- Art Clay Silver – any type of lump, paste or syringe clay can be fired on a gas burner, with a blowtorch or in a kiln; paper clay and oil paste are kiln-fire only.
- PMC3 – any type of PMC3 (lump, slip or syringe) can be fired on a gas burner, with a blowtorch or in a kiln.
- PMC+ – lump, slip and syringe PMC+ clay must be fired with a blowtorch or in a kiln (they cannot be fired on a gas burner); sheet clay is kiln-fire only.

BLOWTORCH FIRING

Blowtorch firing is fast and easy, but many people have not used a blowtorch before and are apprehensive about using one for the first time. The process is not difficult, however, and you will soon enjoy blowtorch firing. All Art Clay Silver, PMC+ and PMC3 clays can be fired with a blowtorch except Paper Type or Sheet clay. You should not use this method for pieces that weigh over 20g or are over 40mm diameter.

yellow flame

STEP 1

Place the dried silver clay on a fire brick. Switch on the torch and adjust the flame to a medium temperature. The fine pencil blue flame is very hot and the yellow flame is cooler. Metal clay should be fired when the tip of the blue flame is just turning yellow – a medium heat.

pencil blue flame

medium flame

MELTING THE PIECE

The only potential problem with blowtorch firing is that you may accidentally melt the metal clay piece if the flame is too intense (this is highly unlikely with the regulated flame on a gas hob). However, you will get plenty of warning of this, so there is time to avoid any major damage. If you see the surface of the silver becoming shiny and silver-coloured, this indicates that you are melting the piece, so simply pull back the flame quickly.

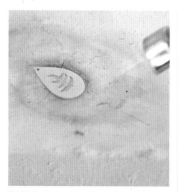

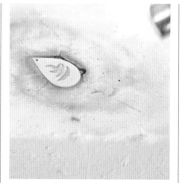

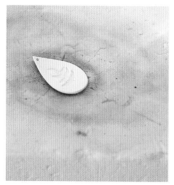

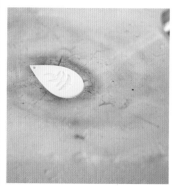

STEP 2

Aim the flame onto the clay so that the piece is entirely in the flame. Move the flame in a circular motion so that the flame is constantly moving over the clay in a stroking action.

STEP 3

After a few moments, a little smoke and flame will show that the binder is burning off. This flame will go out of its own accord. The piece then turns white and you may see it shrink a little.

STEP 4

Sometimes the piece may curl. It usually flattens as firing continues, or you can hammer it after cooling (see page 31).

STEP 5

Wait until the piece glows a pale orange all over and begin timing. One minute is normally enough for most small pieces of clay. Fire for up to 2½ minutes if the piece is larger than 10g. At the end of the time, switch off the torch and either allow the silver to cool for 20 minutes or quench it (see page 29).

KILN FIRING

Any type of metal clay can be fired in a kiln, giving you even more versatility. See chapter 6 for some exciting kiln-fired projects.

STEP 1

Place the metal clay pieces on a firing board. Pieces with a flat back or band rings can be placed directly on the board. Use a fibre cloth to support items that will not lie flat, or set them in vermiculite. Follow the kiln's instructions and set the temperature and time required for the particular type of metal clay you are using (called the 'hold time'). For most kinds of metal clay, you can bring the temperature up to full heat immediately (this is called the 'ramp speed'). Some simple kilns do not have a built-in timer, so you will need to time the pieces with an egg timer once the kiln has reached the temperature required.

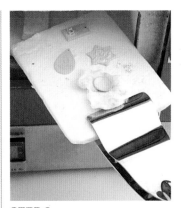

STEP 2

Switch off the kiln and remove the board using tongs and gloves. Allow the silver to cool naturally (about 20 minutes for most jewellery pieces) or quench it.

WHEN TO USE A KILN

While most metal clay jewellery pieces can be fired by other methods, you will need to use a kiln for all of the following:
- Pieces that are larger than the maximum sizes specified for gas burner and blowtorch firing.
- Pieces with fireable gemstones embedded in the clay that are larger than 5mm diameter.
- Metal clay pieces that incorporate glass.
- Pieces made from paper or sheet metal clay, or that incorporate oil paste.
- Hollow-core items made using cork clay and other combustible core materials.

QUENCHING

This is the quickest way to cool fired silver and can be used for all pieces unless they contain other materials, such as gemstones, which should be cooled slowly. See page 107 for cooling glass, which has specific requirements.

Fill a pottery or ceramic bowl with cold water from the tap. Pick up the piece of silver with tweezers and plunge it into the water. You should hear a distinctive hiss if the silver is fresh out of the heat. Beware – if you do not hear the hiss, the silver may not be fully quenched. Dry the silver with a paper towel or cloth. It is now ready for polishing.

SHRINKAGE

After firing by any method, you will find that the piece is a little smaller than it was in the plaster-dry state. All metal clays shrink during firing because the binder burns off and the silver fuses into a solid mass. The amount of shrinkage varies between brands and between clay types. Check the packet to find out the shrinkage. Shrinkage is rarely a problem for pendants, brooches and types of jewellery where size does not matter, but you will need to allow for shrinkage in the following cases:
- Rings must be made a calculated amount bigger to be sure of a correct fit (see page 74).
- If you want to mount a stone into metal clay after firing, you will need to make the mount slightly larger than the stone to start with.
- If you want to replicate a piece from an original by taking a mould (see pages 56–57), be aware that the moulded copy will be smaller.

Finishing techniques

Once the fired metal clay has cooled, it will have a frosty white appearance, because the firing has caused the surface of the silver to become crystalline. This must be smoothed and polished to produce the wonderful shine of pure silver.

BRUSHING

The first stage of finishing fired silver is to brush the frosty surface with a stainless steel brush. A fibreglass brush is a gentler alternative for small or delicate pieces. Brushing gives a satin finish to the silver that looks gorgeous left as it is, or when combined with areas of high mirror polishing. The silver should be dry.

STEP 1
Brush all over the surface of the silver firmly, taking care to keep your fingers away from the brush bristles, which can prick the skin.

STEP 2
Use a small stainless steel brush, or a fibreglass brush for difficult-to-reach areas.

STEP 3
A short-bristled brush is best for the inside of rings.

BURNISHING

This involves rubbing over the surface of the silver to compress it further and produce a shine. It is best used only for textured surfaces or difficult-to-reach nooks and crannies, because it will always leave faint lines on the surface. Use burnishing also for areas around mounted stones, where sanding may cause damage to the stones.

STEP 1
Rub over the surface of the silver with a burnishing tool, taking care not to scratch the silver with the point of the tool. A blunt stainless steel tapestry needle is useful for burnishing tiny areas.

STEP 2
Use a gentler agate tool for delicate burnishing where a stainless steel burnisher would be too aggressive. Silver filigree and gold leaf benefit from this type of burnishing.

FILING

Filing is an excellent way of smoothing and shaping solid silver, and pure silver is the easiest kind to file.

STEP 1

Use a needle file to smooth away any rough areas, using even strokes in one direction only. Pure silver is quite soft and you will find that you can smooth the area remarkably quickly. File marks will be visible on the filed surface, but these will be removed with the subsequent sanding. Use a coarse file for major corrections, and a finer file for small irregularities. Here, the curved side of a half-round needle file is used to file the curved areas inside the bow of a tiny moulded key.

STEP 2

The flat side of a large half-round file is ideal for flat areas. The filed area will look very shiny and have lines marking it from the teeth of the file. If you have used a coarse file, file over the area again with a fine one. Now the piece is ready to be sanded to remove the fine file lines and create a mirror finish (see page 32).

TIPS

Use filing for the following:
- To smooth any rough areas that were missed at the plaster-dry stage.
- To enlarge a ring that is too tight by filing the inside of the shank.
- To remove any sharp edges.
- To smooth areas that have been repaired with oil paste (see page 35).

HAMMERING

Sometimes a piece of metal clay will warp during firing; you can correct this by hammering it gently back into shape. This is only suitable for pieces that have a flat back and no delicate areas. Unless you have a plastic or hide hammer, you will need to protect the piece inside a newspaper or magazine. You can also hammer rings gently on a mandrel if they are not completely round.

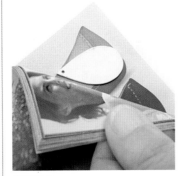

STEP 1

Place the piece between the pages of a magazine to protect the silver surface.

STEP 2

Hammer the piece through several pages of paper – a few firm taps are usually sufficient. The piece should now be flat or you can continue until it is.

MENDING FIRED METAL CLAY

Oil paste is the metal clay worker's solder, and can be used with any kind of fired metal clay. Use it to mend breaks or cracks in fired silver caused by excessive pressure when polishing or stresses during firing, as well as to add findings. Remember that the piece must be refired in a kiln afterwards. Ordinary metal clay paste can be used in the same way and then fired on a gas burner or with a blowtorch, but it is more likely to crack or sheer off. See page 35 for how to use oil paste.

SANDING

Many metal clay pieces are intended to have a mirror finish, but fall well short of it. This is usually because people simply do not rub hard enough when sanding. A mirror finish should be just that – you should be able to see a reflection of your face in the silver. Sanding pads are ideal for this; you can use sandpaper instead, but it is not as easy to get a perfect finish.

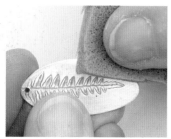

STEP 1
Begin with a superfine (320–600 grit) sanding pad. Rub as firmly as you can on a small area of the silver where you want the mirror shine. (Avoid any textured areas with the pad or you will remove detail.) At first, you will notice a loud rasping noise as the sanding grit bites into the silver. Keep going – after about 30 seconds of hard rubbing, the noise will diminish and you will feel that the pad is slipping over the surface more smoothly. This means that the grit has done its job and that is as far as you can go with that grit.

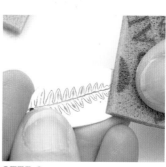

STEP 2
Repeat with an ultrafine (800–1000 grit) sanding pad. Again, you will hear a loud rasping noise that will suddenly quiet down when the grit has smoothed the area fully.

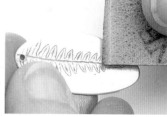

STEP 3
Finally, sand with a microfine (1200–1500 grit) sanding pad. Again, you will hear the noise, but this will drop off quite quickly and the piece will begin to feel really smooth under your fingers. Inspect the sanded surface, which will look slightly satin with tiny lines across it. Now repeat this process over the whole area where you want a mirror finish. The piece is now ready for polishing.

POWER TOOLS

Metal clay pieces can be polished with power tools, such as buffing wheels or a hobby drill with polishing attachments. A rock tumbler is often recommended for polishing metal clay, but it does not produce as high a mirror finish as hand polishing, and should not be used for delicate pieces such as filigree, paste or paper clay.

POLISHING

This is the final stage that will make the silver gleam.

STEP 1
Take a small amount of silver polish on a soft cotton rag or a polishing cloth. Rub over the surface of the silver with a strong pressure. The cloth will turn black where you are rubbing.

STEP 2
Finally, rub the area with a clean part of the cloth. If you have sanded through the grits thoroughly, you will be rewarded with a wonderful mirror shine.

OXIDATION

This is the technique of artificially tarnishing silver with liver of sulphur, and the process can also produce glorious colours. Liver of sulphur is available in lump or liquid form. Use oxidation to antique a piece of silver, to accent engraved and stamped lines with black, or to change the colour of the entire piece. Silver to be oxidized should be mirror polished first if you wish to polish it to bright silver in places.

COLOUR RANGE
The wonderful colour range of liver of sulphur on silver.

STEP 1

Fill a small ceramic cup with hot, but not boiling, water. Add 2–3 drops of liquid liver of sulphur, or a pea-sized piece of the lump form, and stir until fully dissolved. The mixture smells like bad eggs.

STEP 3

Hold the piece with a pair of tweezers and dip it into the solution. Swirl it around so that all parts are exposed to the liquid. After about 10 seconds, pull the piece out to see the progress. Move the tweezers to a new part to avoid being left with an untreated patch and repeat as necessary until you achieve the colour you want.

STEP 5

If you want the piece to have black only in the crevices or lower areas, polish the excess oxidation off the raised parts with silver polish. If you do not like the results, you can easily remove the effects of liver of sulphur by refiring the piece.

STEP 2

Cover the piece of silver in liquid detergent and rub in well to degrease the surface. Rinse thoroughly and now avoid touching it with your fingers.

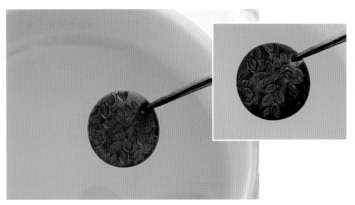

STEP 4

The oxidation begins with a yellowing of the silver and usually proceeds through copper to purple, blue and finally black. You can stop the colour at any point by quickly rinsing the piece in fresh water. The process is rarely predictable and you will have great fun experimenting. The solution will weaken after several pieces have been oxidized, so make a fresh solution as necessary.

TIP

It is best to coat pieces with large areas of colourful oxidation with a varnish of some kind to prevent the effect from rubbing off with wear. Use acrylic or polyurethane varnish, either painted on or sprayed with an aerosol can.

HALLMARKING

Metal clay pieces can be hallmarked as fine silver (999). The law on hallmarking varies from country to country; see page 127 for more information.

Adding findings

TIP

It is best to use pure silver findings when adding them to metal clay before firing, because these will not discolour. Findings made especially for metal clay are available. Sterling silver findings will blacken with firestain when fired because of the copper content of the sterling silver. You can sand the firestain away or use a pickle, a mild acid (this is a silversmithing technique). However, sterling silver findings will not discolour with a low-fire clay that is fired in a kiln at 650°C.

You can add findings to metal clay at all stages. They can be embedded into soft clay, attached with clay paste at the plaster-dry stage or added with oil paste after the clay has been fired. Additional information on adding different types of findings is provided with the projects.

EMBEDDING FINDINGS

Embedding pure silver findings into soft clay is a simple process. Here, screw eyes – tiny loops with a spike – are being embedded into the clay. Screw eyes make small hanging loops for pendants, and attachments for jump rings and wire.

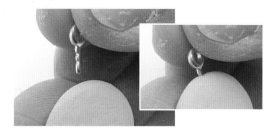

STEP 1
While the clay piece is still soft, push the spike into the clay so that it is embedded up to the loop. Make sure that the entire spike is buried in the clay.

STEP 2
Trim the spike if necessary for embedding into narrow pieces. Alternatively, push the spike in at an angle. Make sure that the clay is snug around the screw eye; if there are any gaps, fill these with paste when the clay is dry or the clay may pull away during firing.

EMBEDDING BEZELS

This is a wonderfully easy way to add faceted gems to a silver piece. Bezels are made to fit a wide variety of stones of different shapes and sizes. Because the stone is added after firing, stones that are not fireable can be added to your jewellery in this way. For embedding stones directly into the clay, see page 61.

STEP 1
Push the bottom of the setting into the clay until the clay surface is level with the base of the upper band. Apply paste to make sure there are no gaps, and clean out any clay inside the setting that might prevent the stone from seating properly.

STEP 2
After firing, place a stone of the correct size and shape into the setting and squeeze the prongs with pliers, alternating opposite sides, to capture the stone.

USING CLAY PASTE

Findings such as bails, screw eyes, brooch findings and loops of silver wire can be attached to plaster-dry clay with paste.

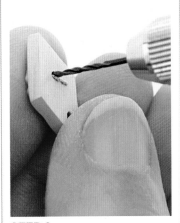

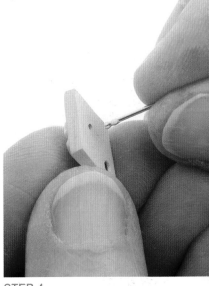

STEP 1
Apply paste to the place where you want to attach the finding, and then press the finding into the paste.

STEP 2
Apply paste over the parts of the finding to be covered. The shape of the finding should be completely invisible under the paste. Dry and sand to smooth the area.

STEP 3
To add posts for earrings or pins for tie tacks, drill a hole in the plaster-dry clay.

STEP 4
Apply paste to the end of the pin and push it into the hole. Paste around the hole to secure, then dry and sand away any excess.

USING OIL PASTE

Use oil paste to attach findings to solid silver, but remember that it must be fired in a kiln afterwards.

STEP 1
Apply oil paste to the surfaces to be joined – here, a bail on the back of a silver leaf. The paste comes with a small bottle of solvent that should be used if the paste is too stiff to spread. Use a cocktail stick to apply the paste, which would ruin a brush. Apply the paste liberally.

STEP 2
Press the bail onto the back of the piece and cover the attachment points with more paste so that their shape cannot be seen. Dry the piece in a domestic oven for 30 minutes at 180ºC. You may need to support it while drying or the join may not hold. Do not attempt to sand the piece before firing or the paste will just flake off. Fire the piece in a kiln according to the manufacturer's instructions. The oil paste will become solid silver, indistinguishable from the surrounding silver clay. When cool, file away any excess.

Basic Projects

This selection of simple beginners' projects is full of appeal. Ranging from pendants to bracelets, they show off the bright patina of pure silver to perfection. The projects are varied so that you can practise all the basic skills of rolling, sculpting, cutting, engraving and polishing.

Impressed pendant

Impressions using proprietary rubber stamps, texture sheets or natural materials are an easy way of decorating metal clay. All you need to do then is cut out a shape to make an attractive pendant.

TIP

Try stamping or impressing onto polymer clay sheets first to see the impressions made by a rubber stamp or texture sheet. Use talcum powder to prevent the stamps from sticking to polymer clay.

LEFT, FROM TOP:
- Stamped fern leaf pendant.
- Pendant impressed with a rubber sheet design, then oxidized and polished back.
- Oxidized skeleton leaf pendant.

RUBBER STAMPS

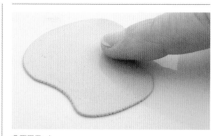

STEP 1
Roll out the clay, 1mm thick, on a non-stick surface and then lay it on a tile. Smear the surface of the clay lightly with vegetable oil to prevent the stamp from sticking in the clay.

STEP 2
Press the stamp firmly into the clay. Check from the side how deeply you are pushing the stamp; it should not be as far as the rubber base or it will make an unwelcome mark.

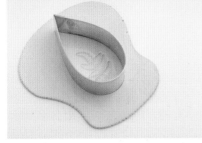

STEP 3

Select a cutter of the appropriate size to cut out the impressed clay. Position the cutter carefully, making sure that the impression is exactly where you want it by looking down into the cutter from above. Try experimenting with asymmetric designs as well as centred ones.

STEP 4

Press the cutter firmly into the clay until it touches the tile. Remove the cutter and pull away the excess clay. The clay piece should not be moved until it is dry to avoid distorting it.

STEP 5

Make a hole for the pendant with a needle tool. This will be refined after drying. Dry the piece thoroughly, then sand gently all around the cut edges. Use a drill bit to refine the hole.

STEP 6

Fire the piece. When cool, brush, sand and polish the smooth areas, and burnish over the impressed areas. Attach the pendant to the chain with a jump ring, using pliers to twist the jump ring open and closed.

RUBBER TEXTURE SHEETS

These can be difficult to position on a small piece of metal clay unless they are transparent. To position, bend the sheet back so that you can see the design you wish to impress and make sure that it is fully over the clay surface. Lay it down on the clay and press over the back of the sheet firmly to make an impression. You may need to make several attempts to find the correct pressure.

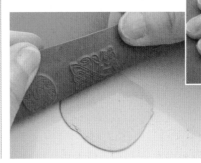

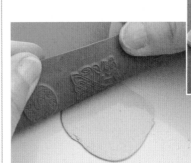

NATURAL TEXTURING MATERIALS

Thin texturing materials, such as leaves, lace and textiles, need to be rolled into the clay. Lay the material onto the rolled out clay sheet. Replace the rolling strips on either side of the clay and roll the texturing material firmly into the clay. Peel off the material. Using rolling strips prevents you from rolling the clay too thinly and ensures a good impression. Fragile materials, such as pressed leaves, may need to be eased out of the clay with the point of a needle.

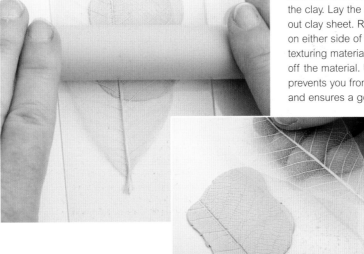

Sculpted doves

Metal clay is perfect for small-scale, one-off sculpture. This appealing jewellery set shows how effective it can be. The sculpting is simple, using basic shapes and textures to create wistful little birds.

PENDANT

STEP 1

Knead the clay and form a 10mm ball for the bird's body. Shape it into a teardrop, with the pointed end for the tail. Press the body down onto a tile to flatten it to about 5mm thick. Form a 6mm ball for the head. Brush the top of the body with water and press the head on, making sure there is a good join.

STEP 2

Form three 3mm balls of clay and roll each into a long teardrop for the tail feathers. Press the tail end of the body a little to flatten it and brush with water. Flatten each teardrop into a feather shape and press them onto the body, pointed end upwards and slightly overlapping.

ABOVE, FROM TOP:
• Dove pendant necklace.
• Dove brooch, made from an enlarged version of the pendant; the eye is embellished with coloured resin.
• Dove earrings, at half the size of the pendant.

TOOLS & MATERIALS

• Basic toolkit
• Silver metal clay: pendant 10g; brooch 10g; earrings 5g
• Silver metal clay paste
• Tools for brushing, sanding, burnishing and polishing
• Pendant findings: pure silver screw eye; silver chain; 5mm silver jump ring
• Sterling silver ear posts and butterflies
• Pure silver brooch finding with sterling silver pin
• 1mm drill bit
• Round nose pliers

STEP 3

Use a craft knife to mark lines on the tail feathers to texture them. Brush the bird with a wet paintbrush to keep it moist and soft while you add the remaining pieces.

STEP 4

Form a 6mm ball for the wing and shape it into a teardrop. Press it with your fingers to flatten it into a wing shape. Brush water on the body and then press the wing on. Mark the upper part with the eye of a needle to suggest feathers and the lower part with lines using a knife.

STEP 5

Roll a small log and point it at one end. Cut off the point for a beak. Brush water onto the front of the head and apply the cut end of the beak. Mark a nostril hole with a needle, pressing the beak onto the clay below to secure it at the same time.

STEP 6

Form a 3mm ball of clay and shape it into a short log for the foot. Press it onto the underside of the body, using the side of the needle to press the centre and curve it around a little. Make a hole for the eye with a large needle.

STEP 7

Dry the piece and use clay paste to attach a screw eye to the back of the base of the head for a good hanging angle. Dry again, then fire, brush, burnish and polish. Using pliers, attach the jump ring to the screw eye and thread it on the chain.

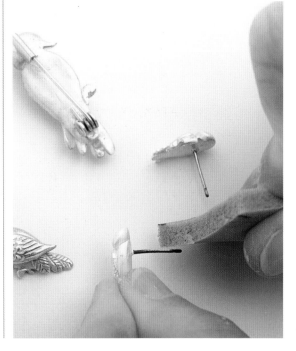

BROOCH AND EARRINGS

Use the same measurements to make a brooch or enlarge it if you wish. After drying, attach the brooch finding to the back of the bird with clay paste. For small stud earrings, halve all the measurements given for the pendant and make two birds facing each other. Dry the pieces, then drill a 1mm hole in the upper back of each piece. Push the end of an ear post into each hole and secure with paste. Dry and fire. The posts have to be sterling silver for strength, so they will darken during firing. Sand the firestain away with sanding pads.

PROJECT 3 | Cutout charm bracelet

Charm bracelets make wonderful gifts, and this dainty version is inspired by the tiny wildflowers found in the high mountains of the Alps. The starting point for each charm is a simple flower cutter. Make as many of each design as you wish.

ABOVE, FROM TOP:
- Vary the arrangement and number of charms in any way you like to complete the bracelet.
- Colour the charms with resin to suggest enamel (see pages 98–99).

TOOLS & MATERIALS
- Basic toolkit
- 10g silver metal clay
- Cutter: simple five-petal flower shape, about 13mm diameter
- Tools for brushing, sanding and burnishing
- Silver chain bracelet
- 5mm silver jump rings; you will need 1 or 2 jump rings per charm
- 1mm drill bit
- Round nose pliers

ROCK ROSE

STEP 1
Roll out the clay, 1mm thick, on a non-stick surface. Cut out a flower shape with the flower cutter.

STEP 2
Lay the cutout flower shape on a finger and press each petal with a paintbrush handle to cup it and shape the petal.

STEP 3
Texture the centre of the flower with little dots using a needle, then mark between each petal with a knife blade to emphasize it.

STEP 4

Use a darning needle to make a hole in one of the petals to hang the flower. This will be enlarged with a drill bit after drying.

ALPINE DAISY

Make in the same way as the rock rose, but cut each petal in two and then use a blunt tapestry needle to cup each of the eight petals.

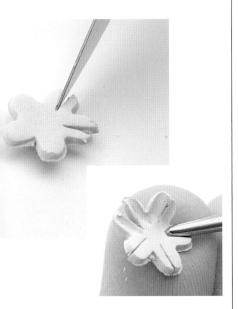

PRIMROSE

Cut out the flower as before, and then scallop each petal by pushing the edge inwards a little with a needle. Cup each petal and define them with a knife blade, then indent the centre of the flower with a blunt needle.

PERIWINKLE

Make a periwinkle in the same way as a primrose, but pinch each petal into a point instead of indenting it.

LEAVES

Form a 6mm ball of clay and shape it into a teardrop. Press it down on a tile to make a leaf shape. (If the clay cracks, it is too dry and needs water added.) Use a knife to mark veins on both sides of the leaf, and pierce a hole for hanging with a needle.

FINISHING AND ASSEMBLY

STEP 1

Dry all the flowers and leaves and refine the pierced holes with a drill bit. Sand lightly over the backs of each flower and sand any rough edges. Fire and then burnish each charm to a shine.

STEP 2

Attach a jump ring to each charm and use this to attach it to a link on the bracelet chain. Space the charms around the bracelet for an attractive effect. You can use two jump rings for some of the charms to make a more varied hang.

Celtic knot pendant

Celtic jewellery is eternally popular. This pendant is based on entwined animal designs in *The Book of Kells*, a medieval manuscript from about 800AD. Use slow-dry clay to give yourself the longest possible working time while tying the knots.

TOOLS & MATERIALS

- Basic toolkit
- 10g slow-dry silver metal clay
- Silver metal clay paste
- Tools for brushing, sanding, polishing and burnishing
- Liver of sulphur
- Silver jump ring, 6mm or larger
- Black rubber necklet or leather thong
- Round nose pliers

TIP

Work with the clay well-moistened, but with the surface dry. If the surface of the clay is wet, it will be slippery and very difficult to hold while you tie the knots.

LEFT, FROM TOP:
- The oxidized pendant looks good hung from black rubber necklet or leather thong.
- Brushed silver that has not been oxidized or polished to a mirror shine combines well with a silver chain.

STEP 1

Divide the clay into three equal pieces. Roll each into a 55mm long log, with one end rounded and the other pointed. Keep the pieces covered with cling film when not working on them.

STEP 2

Position a paintbrush handle or burnishing tool across a log about 3mm from the rounded end, and roll it back and forth to form a snout. Repeat with the other two logs.

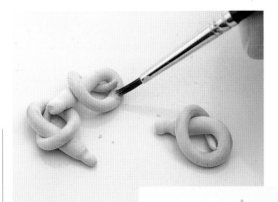

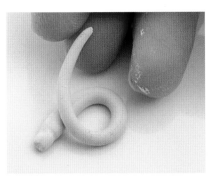

STEP 3

Hold a log with the head end to your left and cross the tail over about 6mm along from the head.

STEP 4

Push the tail end through the loop to make a simple knot. Repeat for the other two logs, tying identical knots. Make sure that you keep the clay moistened but not too wet.

STEP 5

Lay all three knots on a ceramic tile, so that they form a circle with the heads and tails pointing inwards. Brush water onto the body of each, just below where the tail emerges. Ease the knots together, positioning the head and snout of each over the body of the next and pressing to secure.

STEP 6

Use a needle to poke two eyes in each head, on the wider part behind the snout. Pierce right through to the body below to help secure the heads. Pierce smaller holes in the end of each snout for nostrils.

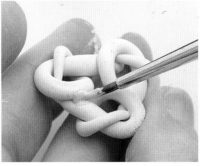

STEP 7

Dry the piece on the tile. When cool, apply paste on the back to make sure that the joins are sound. Dry again, then sand any rough areas. Fire and cool.

STEP 8

Brush, sand and polish the piece, and burnish in the crevices. Using pliers, attach a jump ring through one of the knots. Oxidize the piece with liver of sulphur to give an antique finish, then suspend it from a rubber necklet or leather thong.

Inlaid pendant

Gorgeous coloured inlay is a wonderful complement to the brushed finish of this delicate silver pendant. Polymer clay works beautifully with silver clay and is an easy way to add colour to silver jewellery.

TOOLS & MATERIALS

- Basic toolkit
- 15g slow-dry silver metal clay – this quantity is required for rolling the sheet; less than 7g will be used
- Silver metal clay paste
- Template (see page 125)
- Tracing paper and pencil
- Paper tissue
- Tools for brushing and polishing
- 6mm freshwater pearl bead
- 50cm length of medium-trace sterling silver chain; cut a 13mm piece out of the centre of the chain for attaching the pearl, leaving two equal lengths for attaching to the pendant
- Three 4mm sterling silver jump rings
- 13mm long sterling silver headpin
- 1mm drill bit
- Wire cutters and round nose pliers
- Polymer clay in several colours; pink, leaf green and pearl are used here

LEFT, FROM TOP:
- The sheen of a natural pearl goes beautifully with brushed metal clay.
- This variation features faux semi-precious stones and pearl hearts made from polymer clay.

STEP 1
Trace the template and cut out the shape. Roll out the metal clay two playing cards thick on a tile. Lay the traced template on the clay and cut around it. Remove the scrap clay.

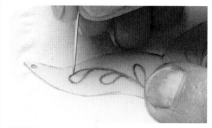

STEP 2
Place the tracing on a folded tissue and prick over the inlay design with a darning needle. This will make embossed pricks on the back of the template. Press the template onto the clay to transfer the prick marks to the clay surface.

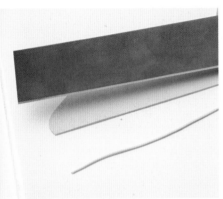

STEP 3

Roll the remaining metal clay into a sheet on a tile, two playing cards thick. Brush the clay surface with water to dampen it, and use a tissue blade to cut a 1mm strip.

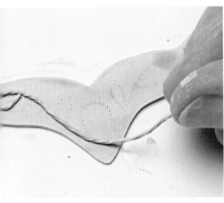

STEP 4

Twist the strip evenly along its length. Dampen the surface of the cutout pendant and lay the twisted strip along the pricked line, coaxing it into position and trimming it to length.

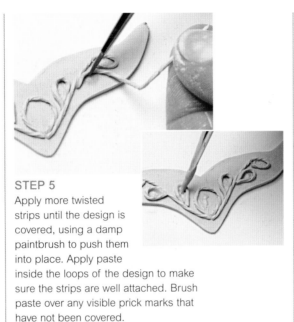

STEP 5

Apply more twisted strips until the design is covered, using a damp paintbrush to push them into place. Apply paste inside the loops of the design to make sure the strips are well attached. Brush paste over any visible prick marks that have not been covered.

STEP 6

Use a needle to make holes at the points indicated on the template. After drying, these will be enlarged with a drill bit. Dry the piece, then sand the upper surface and all around the edges of the piece. Fire, then brush to produce a satin finish.

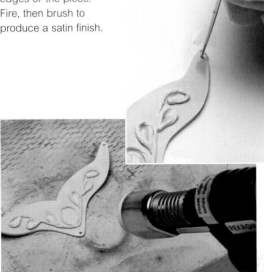

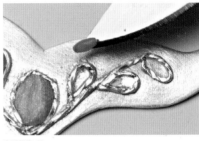

STEP 7

Make small ovals with the polymer clay in the desired colours and press them into the oval cavities of the design. Adjust the amount of polymer clay so that it is level with the top of the twisted strips. Bake the piece in the oven, following the polymer clay baking instructions. Thread the pearl bead onto the headpin. Trim the headpin to 6mm above the bead, form a loop in the end of the wire (see page 59) and add a short length of chain. Use jump rings to attach the three pieces of chain to the drilled holes in the pendant.

ALTERNATIVE FINISH

Use sanding pads to polish the pendant panel around the coloured inlay to a high mirror shine. You will need to use a burnisher to reach the areas closest to the twisted strips.

Dragon brooch

The inspiration for this lovely engraved brooch comes from the dragonesque brooches made by ancient Celtic jewellers. The originals were usually made of bronze and were often decorated with enamel.

TOOLS & MATERIALS

- Basic toolkit
- 15g silver metal clay – this quantity is required for rolling the sheet; less than 10g will be used
- Silver metal clay paste
- Template (see page 125)
- Clear plastic, ballpoint pen or permanent marker and pencil
- Circle cutters or brush protectors: 3mm and 5mm diameter (or use drinking straws)
- Sharp pointed tool for engraving
- Tools for brushing, sanding and polishing
- 55mm long pure silver brooch finding with sterling silver pin
- Fine file
- Wire cutters and round nose pliers

LEFT, FROM TOP:
- Engraved dragon brooch polished to a mirror shine.
- Apply coloured resin to the engraved parts of the design to create the effect of enamelling.
- Oxidize the dragon to the colour of your choice.

STEP 1

Trace the design onto clear plastic with a ballpoint pen or permanent marker and cut out. When laid on the damp clay, this is less likely to curl up and will help keep the clay surface from drying out.

STEP 2

Roll out the clay, 1mm thick, on a non-stick surface and lay on a tile. Place the template on top and use a sharply pointed knife blade to cut out the shape of the dragon. Remove the waste clay and template; do not move the cutout piece.

STEP 3

Impress the smaller circle cutter into the clay to make an impression for each nostril. Repeat with the larger cutter for the two eyes. Push the point of a blunt needle into the centre of each impressed circle. Dry on the tile.

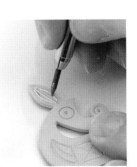

STEP 4

Sand and refine the piece with sanding pads. Draw the central and ear decoration lines onto the clay surface with a pencil, and then use a sharp pointed tool or an engraving tool to engrave the lines onto the piece.

STEP 5

Draw a line on the back of the piece where the brooch finding should go. Position the two parts of the brooch finding on the line and attach with paste. Apply paste over the bases of the findings to secure. Dry thoroughly and sand any rough areas smooth.

STEP 6

Fire the piece. It is relatively large, so if you are firing on a gas burner, you need to make sure that all parts are in the red hot glowing area. Then cool, brush, sand and polish to a mirror shine. The piece has warped a little during firing to give a bowed shape, which could have been hammered out (see page 31), but has been left because it is attractive.

STEP 7

Trim the brooch finding to the correct length with wire cutters and use a fine file to repoint the end.

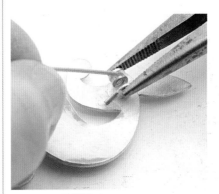

STEP 8

Attach the brooch finding by squeezing its coiled end into the pin base using pliers. The protruding end should slant downwards to provide the spring. The point of the pin should be enclosed entirely in the catch for safety.

Initial pendant

Initial pendants are eternally popular. These charming pendants in copperplate calligraphy designs are not difficult to make. Templates are provided for each letter in the alphabet.

TOOLS & MATERIALS

- Basic toolkit
- 5g slow-dry silver metal clay
- Alcohol or liquid detergent
- Template (see page 124)
- Tracing paper and pencil
- Small sheet of Perspex
- Tools for sanding and brushing; burnishing tools optional
- Silver chain
- Silver jump rings, 6mm or larger
- Round nose pliers

ABOVE:
Oxidize the pendant for an alternative finish.

INITIALS USING ONE LOG

B, C, D, E, H, I, J, L, O, S, T

STEP 1
Clean the tile thoroughly with alcohol or detergent. Trace the initial design onto tracing paper. Scribble with a soft pencil over the back, lay the tracing on the tile and draw firmly over the lines to transfer the letter to the tile.

STEP 2
Use a sheet of Perspex to roll out a 3mm thick log of metal clay. Roll one end of the log into a point and lay that end at the point marked 'A' on the template. Lay the log along the lines of the design, pressing it down lightly onto the tile. Where the log crosses over itself, press the handle of a paintbrush on the lower section to flatten it.

STEP 3
Apply a little water to the flattened area and press the upper section of the log onto it firmly so that it sticks well.

INITIALS WITH A POINTED JOIN

A, G, M, N, U, V, W, Y, Z

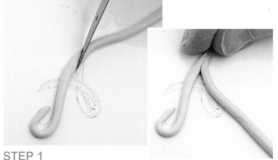

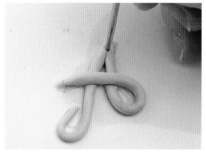

ABOVE, FROM LEFT:
• The A, C and P pendants have been brushed for a satin finish.
• The S, D and R pendants have been polished to a mirror shine.

STEP 1
These initials have a change of direction in the letter that is achieved with a point instead of a loop – marked 'X' on the template. Apply the first log as before and trim the end into a point. Brush water on the cut edge. Press the cut side of the remainder of the log onto it to make a point. Squeeze the point firmly to be sure of a good join. Repeat as necessary to form the letter.

STEP 2
Some of these letters (A, M, N, W) require a hole made in the clay for the jump ring so that they will hang well. To do this, flatten the point where the hole is required and pierce a hole where indicated on the template. Make sure it is big enough to accommodate the jump ring.

STEP 4
When you reach the end of the initial, trim the log into a point. If necessary, use a needle to adjust the log and arrange it into a smooth, flowing shape. Make sure that the loop at the top of the initial is open enough to accommodate the jump ring after firing.

INITIALS USING TWO LOGS

F, K, P, Q, R, X

These are done in the same way as one-log initials, except that a second log is used for part of the letter. Apply the first log and trim the end to a point. Flatten the first log wherever the second log will cross it and brush these areas with water to be sure of good adhesion. Apply the second log, starting at the point marked 'B' on the template. Press firmly where it crosses the first log, then trim and adjust as before.

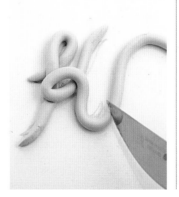

FINISHING

Dry the initial on the tile, then sand and refine the surface gently. Fire the piece. When cool, brush and then burnish or sand the pendant to a high shine.

ASSEMBLY

Using pliers, attach a jump ring either through the loop of the letter or through the hole, depending on the design. Attach the chain.

Liquid silver leaves

When the underside of a real leaf is coated with metal clay paste or slip and then fired, the leaf burns away to leave a replica in solid silver that can be used as a pendant or charm. A tiny polymer clay creature is an optional extra.

TOOLS & MATERIALS

- Basic toolkit
- 10g silver metal clay paste
- Real leaf, about 40mm long with pronounced veins on its underside, such as scented geranium, sage, lemon balm or mint; avoid leaves that are hairy or very thin and limp
- 13mm ball of polymer clay for supporting the leaf; scraps of black and pearl clay for the snail
- Spatula or spade-shaped modelling tool
- Pin vice with 1mm drill bit
- Tools for brushing and burnishing
- Silver chain and jump ring
- Round nose pliers
- Epoxy glue

LEFT, FROM TOP:
- Geranium leaf with polymer clay snail.
- Sage leaf with frog.
- Fern leaf with ladybird.

STEP 1

Scoop a small amount of paste out of the pot onto a tile. Load a paintbrush with water and mix this into the paste to thin it. The ideal mixture will brush easily onto the leaf like a thin cream. If it is too thin, water will separate out while you paint.

STEP 2

Paint the back of the leaf with thinned paste, working the paste into all the crevices until no green is visible.

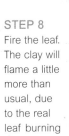

STEP 3

Shape a small tapered log of polymer clay and use it to support the centre of the leaf while you dry the paste for 2 minutes with a hair drier. This will prevent the leaf from flattening out as it dries and gives a more natural shape.

STEP 4

Now that the first layer has been applied thinly to preserve the detail of the leaf surface, you can apply the paste much more thickly. Use a spatula to scoop up undiluted paste and spread it over the leaf. Work cleanly and avoid getting paste on the other side of the leaf.

STEP 5

Dry the paste as before, supported with the polymer clay, and then put another thick layer on the leaf with the spatula. The dried paste should be at least 1mm thick and all the veins should be covered completely. Dry again with the polymer clay support.

STEP 6

Use a paintbrush to build up more paste where needed. Make sure the paste is thick enough at the edges and at the point where you will drill a hole to hang the leaf. Dry the piece.

STEP 7

Check the unpasted side of the leaf for smears of paste, which can spoil the surface of the silver leaf after firing. Clean them away carefully with a cotton bud dipped in water.

STEP 8

Fire the leaf. The clay will flame a little more than usual, due to the real leaf burning away. When cool, drill a hole at a suitable point for hanging. Support the leaf from behind while drilling.

STEP 9

Brush over the leaf carefully with a stainless steel brush. A paste leaf is more fragile than a clay piece of the same thickness, so treat it carefully. Burnish the leaf and attach a jump ring to the hole.

STEP 10

To make a snail, shape a tapered log of black polymer clay, 2mm thick and 10mm long, for the body. Roll up another log of pearl clay for a shell and press it onto the body, curving one end of the body up for a head. Bake following the instructions on the pack and glue with epoxy glue to the silver leaf.

Moulding

Moulding is one of the easiest metal clay techniques, and gives beginners almost instant success. The soft metal clay is pressed into a simple push mould, turned out, trimmed, dried and then fired. This chapter shows how to make your own moulds and then create beautiful moulded pieces in silver.

Making moulds

Polymer clay is ideal for making simple moulds with low relief, while silicone can be used for more three-dimensional objects and for items that are too fragile to be pressed into polymer clay.

found object   mould made from polymer clay   silver clay facsimile cast from mould

POLYMER CLAY MOULDS

Polymer clay is very easy to work with. Premo Sculpey is the best type to use for making moulds.

STEP 1
Break off a piece of polymer clay that is large enough to mould the item you have chosen, and knead until it is soft. Form it into an oval shape and press it down onto a tile to make a patty that is at least double the depth of the item you want to mould and large enough to take the impression.

STEP 2
Smooth a thin coat of talcum powder over the surface of the clay disc and press the item, face down, smoothly into the clay. If you are moulding a button, stop pressing when the back of the button is level with the surface of the clay.

STEP 3
Use the point of a needle to ease up one edge of the moulded item and remove it from the clay. Do not attempt to move the clay mould. Instead, place the tile, with the clay on it, directly into the oven and bake as instructed on the polymer clay packet – usually about 20 minutes at 130°C. Cool the piece and remove from the tile.

TOOLS & MATERIALS

- 56g white polymer clay
- Ceramic tile
- Talcum powder
- Objects for moulding
- Needle or needle tool
- Craft knife

SILICONE MOULDS

The flexibility of a silicone mould means that you can create a certain amount of undercutting, because the mould can be flexed to remove the metal clay.

TOOLS & MATERIALS

- Putty silicone moulding compound
- Objects for moulding

STEP 1

Scoop out equal quantities of each of the two colours of silicone moulding compound. Take care not to contaminate each pot with the other colour.

TIPS

- Start a collection of novelty buttons, small toys and items of jewellery for making moulds.
- Use natural objects, such as shells, leaves, seeds and nuts.
- Make moulds from the relief mouldings on picture frames.
- Proprietary moulds are widely available for use with clays.

STEP 2

Knead the two parts together until the colour is even. The silicone is now ready to use.

STEP 3

Shape the silicone into a ball and flatten to make a small patty, larger all around than the object you intend to mould. Press the object onto the patty, pushing the silicone just over halfway up the sides; make sure that there are no gaps.

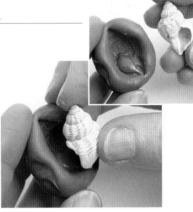

STEP 4

Allow the putty to set with the object in place. This usually takes about 5–10 minutes. You can test the silicone with a fingernail; it has hardened when you cannot make a mark. Flex the silicone and pop out the object. The mould is now ready for use.

MOULDING FRAGILE ITEMS

Silicone can be used to make moulds from delicate objects, such as blackberries, because the soft silicone will not squash the berries when moulding them.

Key charm necklace

These tiny keys come from old jewellery boxes, cabinets and other small pieces of furniture. Similar ones are often to be found in antique or second-hand shops. They make delightful jewellery, and would be particularly apt for a 21st birthday gift.

TOOLS & MATERIALS

- Basic toolkit
- Silver metal clay; you will need about 5g for a 25mm long key
- Small decorative keys, about 25–30mm long
- Polymer clay and talcum powder for moulding
- Vegetable oil
- Small circle cutter, such as a brush protector or drinking straw
- Tools for filing, sanding, brushing, burnishing and polishing
- Silver chain with links large enough to attach jump rings
- Four 5mm and three 8mm sterling silver jump rings
- Four 30mm long sterling silver headpins
- Four 13mm blue-green glass tube beads
- Eight 3mm silver-coloured round glass beads
- Wire cutters and round nose pliers

LEFT, FROM TOP:
- Three different key designs alternated with beaded drops.
- A single moulded key on a necklace of pearl beads.

STEP 1

Make polymer clay moulds for the keys (see page 56). Press each key into the clay about halfway up the sides of the key. The keys can be baked in the moulds and removed afterwards, because the oven heat will not harm them.

STEP 2

Knead a piece of metal clay and form into a log that is about the same size as the key to be

moulded. Smear a light coating of oil onto the clay surface and press the clay into the mould. Work firmly with your finger, pushing the clay into all the crevices and completely filling the mould cavity.

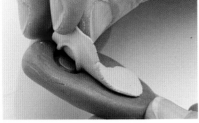

STEP 3

Trim away some of the excess clay if it is too high above the mould surface, but leave a thin tag of it to provide a handle to pull the clay out of the mould. Use the tag to ease the clay gently out of the mould.

STEP 4

Lay the piece face up on a tile. Use a knife to trim away the excess clay all around the key and save it to use for another project.

STEP 5

Use a small circle cutter to cut out the clay inside the key's top loop. It is not necessary to trim completely; it will be easier to file away any remaining excess after the piece is dried.

STEP 6

Dry the piece and then use files and sandpaper to refine the key shape further. Smooth the back well, because it may be visible when worn. You can curve the key shank around to the back with a file to make it reversible.

STEP 7

Repeat to make two more keys and then fire them all. When cool, brush, burnish and polish the keys. File away any sharp edges.

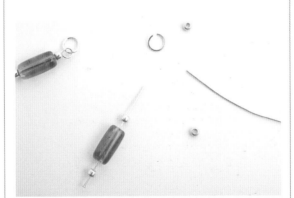

STEP 8

Thread each headpin with a silver bead, a glass bead and another silver bead. Trim each headpin to 6mm above the final bead, make a loop in the end of the wire, and add a small jump ring.

STEP 9

Lay the chain so that all the links lie in the same way and find the centre link. Attach the largest key to this with a large jump ring. Attach a beaded headpin to the chain on either side of the central key. Working outwards and making sure they are spaced symmetrically, add another key and beaded headpin on either side of the central key.

MAKING A WIRE LOOP

Grip the end of the wire with round nose pliers and turn the pliers to form a loop. Remove the pliers and grip the loop at its base. Turn the pliers back a little to kink the wire at the base of the loop so that the loop lies in the centre of the wire.

Gem-studded tie tack

This stylish tie tack is set with a fireable gemstone and makes a great gift. A tiny charm is used to make the embossed crown embellishment in a technique borrowed from ceramics called 'sprigging'. If you cannot find a suitable charm, then a small herb leaf can be used instead to make the mould.

TOOLS & MATERIALS

- Basic toolkit
- 7g silver metal clay
- Silver metal clay paste
- Small charm, about 10mm across or less
- Polymer clay and talcum powder for moulding
- Vegetable oil
- 13–20mm square or round cutter
- Tools for sanding, brushing, polishing and burnishing
- 3mm round cubic zirconia or other fireable artificial gemstone
- Tie tack finding
- 1mm drill bit

LEFT, FROM TOP:
- Tie tack with crown motif and deep blue gemstone.
- Vary the tie tack by changing the colour of the gemstone, the shape of the cutter used and the design of the moulded motif.

STEP 1

Roll out a 3mm thick sheet of polymer clay on a non-stick surface. It should be at least 30mm across. Lay the sheet on a tile, brush the surface with talc and lay the charm, face down, in the centre of the clay. Roll again to impress the charm into the clay surface and keep the surrounding clay as smooth as possible.

STEP 2

Bake the polymer clay on the tile following the manufacturer's instructions (if the charm is metal, it can be left in place until after baking). When cool, sand over the surface to ensure it is completely smooth.

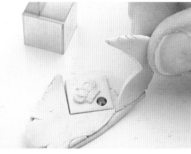

STEP 3

Form a small ball of metal clay, about the same size as the mould cavity. Smear a thin coating of oil over the ball and press it into the cavity. Keep pressing to make sure that the clay is forced into all the crevices, then use a knife to slice away all the excess clay above the surface of the mould cavity.

STEP 4

Roll out a 3mm thick sheet of metal clay. Brush the back of the clay in the mould cavity with water to make sure it will stick well to the clay sheet. Centre the clay sheet over the mould and press down firmly.

STEP 5

Lightly wet the back of the clay sheet so that it will stick to the tile. Flip the mould and sheet so that the clay is underneath and press both down onto the tile to flatten the back of the sheet. Carefully lift the mould off the clay.

STEP 6

Hold a large needle over the point where you wish to insert the stone. Press down until it touches the tile below, and then rotate it in a circular motion to enlarge the hole to just under 3mm across.

STEP 7

Pick up the stone with tweezers and place it in the hole. Use a needle to push it down into the clay so that the flat top of the stone is level with the clay surface. This is a neat way of setting stones in soft clay.

STEP 8

Cut out the tie tack shape using the cutter, taking care that the embossed motif and gemstone are aligned and the gemstone is at least 3mm from the edge. Remove the waste clay from around the piece and dry on the tile.

STEP 9

Sand around the motif and stone. Use a drill bit to make a hole in the back, about 2mm deep, for the tie tack finding, and secure this in the hole with paste.

STEP10

Fire the tie tack, then brush, sand and polish it. Burnish the area around the motif and the motif itself. The tie tack pin is not pure silver, so it will have blackened and will need to be sanded to clean it.

PROJECT 11 ❙ Acorn cufflinks

A real acorn is used here to make a sparkling pair of cufflinks. Choose a small acorn 2.5cm long or less, so that the cufflinks are not too heavy when worn. If you cannot find an acorn, use a similar shaped object, such as a small seashell or a novelty button.

ABOVE:
Make a matching tie tack to go with the acorn cufflinks.

TOOLS & MATERIALS

- Basic toolkit
- Silver metal clay; 10g is enough for two 20mm long acorn cufflinks
- Silver metal clay paste
- Acorn for moulding
- Putty silicone moulding compound
- Hair drier or heat gun
- 1mm drill bit
- Four 6mm lengths of 0.8mm pure silver wire with a loop at one end of each length (see page 59)
- Four 4mm sterling silver jump rings
- Tools for brushing, sanding, burnishing and polishing
- Two 13mm lengths of silver chain
- Round nose pliers

STEP 1
Make a silicone mould of the acorn (see page 57).

STEP 2
Knead the metal clay and form a smooth ball to fit into the mould. Push the ball into the mould, pressing firmly so that the clay is pushed into all parts of the mould and the exposed surface is smooth and flat.

OPPOSITE, FROM LEFT:
• Acorn cufflinks.
• Use other found objects, such as a tiny pinecone, to mould a pair of cufflinks.

STEP 3

If there is excess clay, slice it off with a craft knife. Smooth the surface of the clay again; smoothing it now will save work later. Dry the piece for a minute or two with a hair drier or for about 30 seconds with a heat gun to part-dry the clay and make it easier to unmould without distortion.

STEP 4

Flex the mould to remove the clay acorn. The clay should be hard enough to hold its shape as you remove it from the mould, but if it shows signs of distorting, dry it for a little longer. Repeat to make a second acorn.

STEP 5

Form a 1.5mm thick log of clay and cut two 13mm lengths for the stalks. Make a hole in the top of each acorn with a thick needle (or use a drill bit if the clay is too dry). Stick the end of a stalk into each hole, using paste to attach it. Curve each stalk using your fingers.

STEP 6

Roll a 5mm thick log of clay and cut two 2cm lengths for the cufflink toggles. Make a shallow hole in the centre of one side of each with a needle. Dry all the pieces thoroughly and allow to cool.

STEP 7

Sand the backs of the acorns and all over the cufflink toggles to smooth them. Use a drill bit to make a hole in the centre back of each acorn and enlarge the hole in the centre of each toggle.

STEP 8

Use paste to attach the wire loops into the drilled holes. Make sure that the loops are well embedded in the clay for strength. Dry again and then fire.

STEP 9

Brush, burnish, sand and polish all the pieces. Burnish the loops to make them stronger. Using pliers, attach a length of chain to each acorn back and toggle with jump rings.

Beads & Rings

Beads are always popular, and what a delight it is to create your own pure silver beads to make into necklaces, bracelets and earrings. Ring making is a great favourite with many people, and the projects that follow cover a lively collection of different styles to suit everyone's tastes.

Beads without a kiln

The traditional way to make hollow forms or beads in metal clay is to use a core material, such as cork clay, that burns away when fired. A kiln is advisable for this technique because of the toxic fumes produced. However, the use of formers and moulds can produce excellent beads that can be fired on a gas burner or with a blowtorch.

TOOLS & MATERIALS

- Basic toolkit
- 10g silver metal clay
- Silver metal clay paste
- Vegetable oil
- Two 25mm marbles
- Scrap of polymer clay
- 25mm circle cutter
- Rubber stamp with small motif
- Tools for filing, sanding, brushing and polishing

LENTIL BEADS

Using a marble as a former to make beads in two halves produces excellent results. A lentil shape is the easiest type of bead to make on a marble. You can vary the size according to the size of marble and cutter you use. The bead shown is decorated with a rubber stamp; the following pages give additional ideas.

STEP 1

Use a small piece of polymer clay to hold a marble in place on a tile. Roll out the metal clay 1mm thick and cut out a circle with a cutter. Smear a sparing amount of vegetable oil onto the top of the marble. The glass should be just greasy, but not slippery. This will help you when removing the dry clay later.

STEP 2

Press a clay circle onto the top of the marble, smoothing the edges down the sides. The clay should not reach more than halfway down the sides of the marble or it will be difficult to remove.

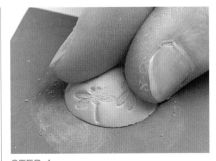

STEP 4

Hold each half, cup side down, on a piece of sandpaper and rotate it gently to smooth the edge. Keep checking that the two halves will match and sand until they do.

STEP 6

Apply paste liberally around the edge of one half-bead, then press the two halves together. Add more paste around the join to cover any signs of it, but keep the holes clear.

STEP 3

Rub a little vegetable oil on the stamp and press the stamp onto the clay, repeating the motif evenly over the half-bead. Repeat to make a second half-bead. Dry the clay thoroughly on the marbles. Allow to cool and then twist each half-bead off its marble. If it will not come off easily, run a knife around the edge to help it off and use more oil next time.

STEP 5

Hold the edge of a file across the centre of one half-bead and file grooves in the clay. If you want the bead to hang as a feature bead, make the groove just above the halfway mark.

STEP 7

Dry thoroughly and then sand smooth. Fire the bead, then brush, sand or burnish, and polish.

MOULDED BEADS

Instead of making beads on a marble, you can make half-bead moulds from purchased beads and use these to mould metal clay bead halves to be joined together.

- Basic toolkit
- 10g silver metal clay
- Beads for moulding – glass, metal, ceramic, wood, etc
- Putty silicone moulding compound
- Pencil with eraser on the end or similar blunt tool
- Drill bit – size depends on size of hole required
- Tools for filing, sanding, brushing and polishing

STEP 1

Make a mould of each bead from the moulding compound so that the bead is pushed into the compound just over halfway (see page 57).

STEP 2

Make a pancake shape from the metal clay, about 2mm thick and large enough to cover the mould cavity. Use the eraser end of a pencil to push the clay into the bottom of the mould cavity and up the sides. Trim the clay around the edges of the mould with a knife. Dry and unmould (see page 63).

STEP 3

When fully dry, sand the bead halves, drill holes where required, and finish as for lentil beads (see pages 66–67).

TUBE BEADS

- Basic toolkit
- 10g silver metal clay
- Silver metal clay paste
- Vegetable oil
- 10mm metal or plastic knitting needle
- Tissue blade
- Modelling tool with a blunt end
- Drill bit – size depends on size of hole required
- Tools for sanding, brushing and polishing

These are quick to make and can be used as beautiful feature beads. The instructions here are for making a bead 40mm long and about 13mm thick, but you can vary the size by using different sized knitting needles as formers.

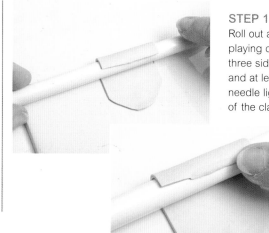

STEP 1

Roll out a sheet of metal clay three playing cards thick. Cut the sheet to make three sides of a rectangle, 40mm wide and at least 50mm long. Smear a knitting needle lightly with oil. Lay the cut end of the clay sheet on the knitting needle and press along the edge to chamfer it.

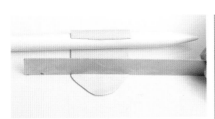

STEP 2

Roll up the knitting needle in the clay until the first edge meets the clay again; it will make a slight line. Unroll and cut just beyond the line with a tissue blade.

STEP 3

Press this cut edge onto a non-stick work surface to chamfer it. This will help to make a neat overlapping join.

STEP 4

Apply a line of paste on the cut edge and press the first edge onto it.

STEP 5

Use a tool to smooth the clay join. Leave the join thicker than the surrounding clay, because it will be easier to sand it smooth when dry. Partially dry the clay on the knitting needle (if using a heat gun and the needle is plastic, take care to aim the gun at the clay and not the needle or it may melt).

STEP 6

When the clay is cool enough, grasp it in one hand and twist the needle with the other to remove the clay tube bead from the needle.

STEP 7

Dry the bead. Lay a piece of sandpaper on the work surface and rub each end of the bead on the sandpaper to smooth and straighten it.
Sand the join smooth with a superfine sanding pad.

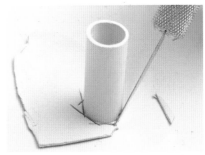

STEP 8

To make the bead ends, roll out another sheet of clay to the same thickness and lay it on a tile. Apply paste generously to one end of the bead and press it down onto the clay sheet. Trim the excess clay all around the bead. Dry until the bead can be removed from the tile and then repeat at the other end.

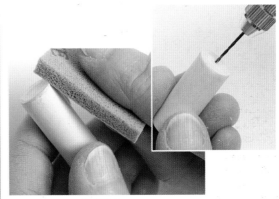

STEP 9

Dry the bead thoroughly and then sand the joins at the ends smooth. Drill a hole in the centre of each end (the size of drill bit depends on the thickness of the cord you plan to use). Fire, allow to cool, then brush, sand and polish. You can decorate the bead in many different ways, such as an engraved design.

Treasure bead bracelet

This colourful bracelet is made using different kinds of silver and glass beads for a lovely eclectic look. The finished bracelet is 20cm long, but you can add or subtract beads to alter the length.

TOOLS & MATERIALS

- Basic toolkit
- 20g silver metal clay (quantity depends on size and number of beads)
- Silver metal clay paste
- Vegetable oil
- Two 15mm marbles
- Scrap of polymer clay
- 20mm circle cutter
- Rubber stamp with small motif
- Brass paper-embossing stencil with small motif
- 5mm knitting needle
- Silicone half-bead mould made from a 20mm long oval glass bead (see pages 57 and 68)
- Tissue blade
- Modelling tool with a blunt end
- Tools for filing, sanding, brushing and polishing
- Pin vice with 1mm drill bit
- Five 6mm glass or crystal beads
- 30cm length of 0.8mm sterling silver wire
- Clasp and two 5mm sterling silver jump rings
- Wire cutters and round nose pliers

LEFT, FROM TOP:
- Alternate silver and pastel-coloured glass beads for a delicate look.
- Oxidize the silver beads and then polish back the raised areas to accentuate the patterns of the designs.

STEP 1
Use a circle cutter and two marbles to form the two halves of the first lentil bead, decorating each half evenly with impressions from a rubber stamp (see pages 66–67). Dry the bead halves on the marbles, then remove them to make a second bead.

STEP 2
Make the two halves of a second lentil bead, but this time decorate them with an embossing stencil. Press one of the stencil motifs onto the clay just hard enough for the clay to bulge through the stencil. You will need to rock the stencil sheet to make sure that the edges of the motif are fully pressed into the clay.

STEP 3

Remove the stencil sheet. The resulting impression should show the motif embossed in the soft clay. Repeat to impress the motif evenly around each half-bead. Dry the bead halves on the marbles. Finish both lentil beads, filing a hole before joining the halves.

STEP 4

Make two 20mm long tube beads; dry and sand smooth (see pages 68–69). Draw a scattering of stars over one of the beads with a pencil. File a line across the centre of each star using the edge of a file, then file across the line twice more.

STEP 5

Mark diagonal lines on the other tube bead with a pencil. File along the lines with the edge of the file. Drill holes in the ends of both tube beads.

STEP 6

Use a silicone mould to make two halves of a plain oval silver bead, drilling a hole in each end of the finished bead. Fire all the beads. When cool, leave the oval bead with a matt finish and mirror polish the remaining beads.

STEP 7

Form a loop in the end of the wire (see page 59) and thread on a bead. Trim the wire to 6mm from the bead and form another loop. Repeat for all the other beads. Link all the beads together by joining the loops, alternating the silver beads with the glass ones.

STEP 8

Attach a jump ring to the loop at each end of the bracelet, and then attach a clasp to one of the jump rings.

Celtic bead necklace

An antiqued silver tube bead with a Celtic pattern is set off with gossamer-fine organza ribbons in this unusual necklace.

TOOLS & MATERIALS

- Basic toolkit
- 15g silver metal clay – this quantity is required for rolling the sheet; only about 10g will be used
- Silver metal clay paste
- Vegetable oil
- Rubber texture sheet
- 10mm knitting needle
- Tissue blade
- 13mm circle cutter
- 2mm drill bit
- Tools for brushing, sanding and polishing
- Liver of sulphur
- Three 45cm lengths of 4mm wide organza ribbon in purple, plum and emerald green
- Two sterling silver spring ends with loops
- Sterling silver hook
- Round nose pliers

STEP 1

Roll out the clay three playing cards thick and lay on a non-stick surface. Smear lightly with vegetable oil and use a rubber texture sheet to impress a pattern onto the clay surface. Here, a border pattern has been impressed repeatedly on the diagonal.

STEP 2

Referring to the instructions on pages 68–69, cut a rectangle 40mm wide and at least 50mm long and form a tube bead around a knitting needle. Trim the ends with a tissue blade, then dry and remove from the needle. Sand the ends and the join.

STEP 3

Roll out more clay, three playing cards thick and cut out two circles with a circle cutter. Apply paste to the ends of the bead and press on the clay circles. Dry, sand any rough edges and then drill holes in the ends with a drill bit.

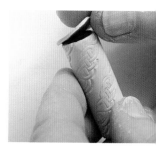

STEP 4

Fire and polish the bead, then oxidize it with liver of sulphur. Polish back to accentuate the pattern. Thread a large darning needle with the three ribbons together and thread on the bead, tying a knot in the ribbons above and below the bead to secure it. Trim the ribbons to the same length on either side of the bead. Thread one end through a spring end, tie the end in a knot and pull the knot back into the spring end. Using pliers, squeeze the bottom coil to hold the knot securely. Repeat for the other end of the ribbons and attach a hook.

PROJECT 14 | Moroccan lamp earrings

These exotic earrings are inspired by the gorgeous brass and silver lamps found in North Africa. Tiny cutters are used to decorate lentil beads, simulating the pierced metal of the lamps.

TOOLS & MATERIALS

- Basic toolkit
- 7g silver metal clay
- Silver metal clay paste
- Vegetable oil
- Four 15mm marbles
- Scrap of polymer clay
- 20mm circle cutter and 5mm heart cutter
- Pin vice with 1mm drill bit
- Tools for filing, brushing, sanding and polishing
- Ball tool for burnishing
- Two 8mm and two 3mm red glass beads
- Two 50mm long sterling silver eyepins
- 15cm length of sterling silver chain
- Eight 5mm sterling silver jump rings
- Two sterling silver fish hook earwires
- Wire cutters and round nose pliers

STEP 1
Make four lentil half-beads (see pages 66–67). While the soft clay is on the marble, use a heart cutter to cut out four hearts evenly around each half-bead. Use a needle to lever out the waste clay. Complete the beads in the usual way, but drill a hole in the centre of each half-bead rather than across it.

STEP 2
Roll out a sheet of the remaining clay, 1mm thick, and place on a tile. Cut out six hearts and pierce each with a needle. Dry on the tile and redrill the holes with the drill bit. Sand smooth.

STEP 3
Fire the beads and hearts. Brush, sand and polish the beads to a mirror finish. Push a ball tool through the pierced hearts to burnish inside.

STEP 4
Thread each bead onto an eyepin and then thread on a large and then a small red bead. Trim the pin to 6mm above the top of the small bead and form a loop (see page 59). Attach an earwire to the top loop.

STEP 5
Cut the chain into two of each of the following lengths: 30mm, 25mm and 15mm. Attach a jump ring to the bottom loop of each eyepin and to three lengths of chain. Use the remaining jump rings to attach the hearts to the end of each chain.

Making rings

Ring making is one of the most exciting aspects of using metal clay, because it enables the home crafter to make pure silver rings at home. The following pages show you how to make a variety of rings, from the simple to the more advanced – and how to get them to fit.

SIZE GUIDE

The following chart gives a rough guide for the amount of allowance required for clay shrinkage (see box), depending on the shape of ring you are making. Use a ring gauge to measure the finger or an existing ring, and add the amount specified. These amounts are for clays that shrink around 8–10 per cent. Add an extra ¼–½ size for clay with shrinkage of 12 per cent or more. Note that different countries have different ring-sizing systems.

RING SHAPE	US & CANADA A: sizes 6–10 B: sizes 11 and above	UK & AUSTRALASIA A: sizes K–S B: sizes T and above	JAPAN A: sizes 10–20 B: sizes 21 and above
Slim round shank – 3mm thick or less	A: add 1 size B: add 1 size	A: add 2 sizes B: add 2½ sizes	A: add 2 sizes B: add 3–4 sizes
Flat band ring with shank at least 6mm wide and approximately 1–1.5mm thick	A: add 1 size B: add 1¼ sizes	A: add 2 sizes B: add 2½ sizes	A: add 2½ sizes B: add 3½–4½ sizes
Heavy ring with a shank 20mm wide and 3mm thick or more	A: add 1¼ sizes B: add 1½–2 sizes	A: add 2½ sizes B: add 3½–4½ sizes	A: add 3 sizes B: add 4–5 sizes

slim round shank

flat shank

heavy shank

PREPARING A RING MANDREL

Metal clay rings can be made on a simple, inexpensive wooden mandrel.

STEP 1

Measure the finger with a ring gauge. Most people will find that there are three sizes that are all comfortable, so locate these and use the central size.

TOOLS & MATERIALS

- Ring mandrel
- Ring sizing gauge or card
- Pencil and ruler
- 10cm long sticky note

TIP

The problems of shrinkage make the sizing of rings made with metal clay more an art than a science. If you are a beginner, a good idea is to make your first ring for a middle finger – so there is a finger on either side to wear the ring if you get it wrong.

STEP 2

Add the appropriate number of sizes, referring to the chart opposite. Slide the appropriate ring gauge down onto the mandrel as far as it will go, then mark the mandrel with a pencil at that point.

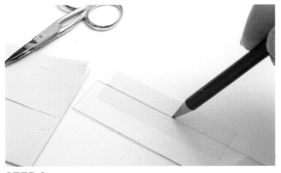

STEP 3

Cut a 2.5cm wide strip from a sticky note, making sure that the sticky part is at one end of the strip for securing it to the mandrel. Draw a line down the centre of the non-sticky side of the paper as a guideline.

STEP 4

Lay the pencil line drawn on the centre of the strip across the marked line on the mandrel. Wrap the strip around the mandrel, securing it with the sticky end of the strip over the other end.

STEP 5

The strip needs to be snug on the mandrel, but check that you can still slide it off the mandrel when required. The mandrel is now ready to use. The sticky note will prevent the wet clay from sticking to the mandrel.

PROJECT 15 | Classic band ring

TOOLS & MATERIALS

- Basic toolkit
- Silver metal clay –
  7g for an average-size
  woman's ring; 10g or
  more for a man's ring
- Silver metal clay paste
- Prepared ring
  mandrel with allowance
  for shrinkage (see
  page 75)
- Graph paper and pencil
- Tissue blade
- Modelling tool with a
  blunt end
- Hair drier and baking
  sheet
- Template (see
  page 125)
- Tracing paper
- Engraving tool
- Tools for sanding,
  brushing and polishing
- Liver of sulphur

This timeless ring is a basic shape that can be left plain if you wish or decorated in a fantastic variety of ways. The engraved design shown here gives a classic beauty to the ring. It is not difficult to achieve if you take your time and support the ring as you engrave the plaster-dry surface.

STEP 1

To measure how long to make the strip of clay, cut a strip of graph paper 10mm wide and at least 5cm long, using the grid lines to help. Wrap it around the central guideline on the sticky note wrapped around the mandrel. Mark where it meets and add about 6mm. Trim it at this point.

STEP 2

Shape the clay into a log and roll it flat into a long strip, 1mm thick, on a non-stick surface. Lay the graph paper on the clay and use a tissue blade to cut out the strip of clay. Flatten the ends of the strip to chamfer them.

STEP 3

Wet a finger and apply a thin film of water to the top of the clay strip. Lift up the clay and apply it, wet side down, to the sticky note on the mandrel. The wet clay should stick to the paper so that it is easier to control. Keep the strip as straight as you can on the mandrel.

RIGHT:
- Wide ring engraved with leaf decoration.
- A narrower leaf-engraved variation for a smaller hand.

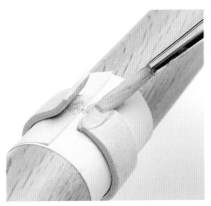

STEP 4

The beveled ends of the strip should overlap each other by about 3mm, so trim one end if necessary and then flatten again. Apply some paste to one end and press the other end onto it, pressing firmly to make a good join.

STEP 5

Smooth the join – it should be thicker than the rest of the ring; this will be corrected when it is plaster-dry. Check that the strip is in contact with the paper all around; if |it is loose, cut it and join again or the ring will be too big. If the join shows as a line, cover it with a coat of paste.

STEP 6

Dry the ring on the mandrel with a hair drier (do not use a heat gun, because it is too hot for the wooden mandrel). Carefully remove the ring, still on the sticky note, and stand it on end on a baking sheet. Dry thoroughly.

STEP 7

Carefully remove the sticky note from inside the ring by pushing the paper gently away from the ring shank all around and then folding it in on itself and pulling it out.

STEP 8

Use a superfine sanding pad to sand all around the outside of the ring, sanding more over the join so that the ring is the same thickness throughout. Hold the ring on its side on some sandpaper and sand with a circular motion to straighten the edges. Sand inside the ring with a roll of sandpaper, and bevel the inner edge to make it more comfortable to wear. Fill any cracks or dents with paste, dry and then sand again.

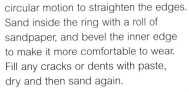

STEP 9

Copy or trace the wavy leaf design onto the ring with a pencil. Supporting the ring

carefully inside, or working with it on the mandrel, use an engraving or other pointed tool to engrave the design. Take care to support the point behind where you are engraving and take care not to put pressure inadvertently on the other side of the ring. If the ring cracks, you can mend it with paste.

STEP 10

Fire the ring. When cool, brush with a stainless steel brush, using a short-bristled brush for the inside of the ring. Sand and polish to a mirror finish. To emphasize the engraving, oxidize the ring with liver of sulphur and then polish back the surface area.

PROJECT 16 ┃ Jewelled ring

An elegant solitaire stone gives this ring wide appeal. The shank is made from pure silver wire to avoid the complications of metal clay shrinkage and sizing – the ring is simply made in the correct size.

ABOVE, FROM LEFT:
- Ruby stone in a double-diamond setting.
- Vary the colour of the stone for a different look.

BELOW:
- Wrap straight, untwisted wire around the mandrel several times to form a shank, and use an alpine daisy setting for the stone (see page 43).

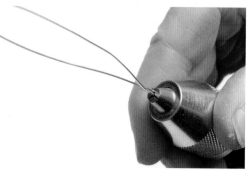

STEP 1
To make the shank, bend the wire in half and clamp the two ends tightly in the chuck of a hand drill. Hook the other end of the wire over something solid, such as a door handle, or a G-clamp attached to a heavy table.

STEP 2
Wind the handle of the drill so that the wire twists into an even rope. Continue until the wire is fairly tightly twisted. Remove it from the drill and the door handle.

STEP 5

Form a 6mm ball of clay into an oval and press this down on the gap in the wire to cover the gap and the ends of the wire. Press down firmly until the top of the clay is level with the top of the wire. Trim the sides of the clay level with the wire. This will be the base on which you will create the ring setting.

STEP 6

Roll out a 1mm thick sheet of clay and cut out a diamond with a cutter. Apply paste to the clay join on the ring shank and press on the diamond shape, so that the longer points are in line with the wire and the shorter points curve around slightly to touch the paper.

STEP 7

Brush the diamond shape with water to keep it soft. Cut out another diamond shape and trim off 3mm from two edges on one side to make a smaller diamond of clay.

STEP 8

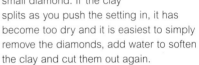

Apply paste to the larger diamond and press the smaller one onto the centre of it, aligning the points carefully. Now press the bezel, angled so that it continues the diamond effect, into the centre of the small diamond. If the clay splits as you push the setting in, it has become too dry and it is easiest to simply remove the diamonds, add water to soften the clay and cut them out again.

STEP 9

Dry the ring and remove from the paper (see steps 6–7, page 77). Apply paste liberally to the join under the ring setting, making sure that the ends of the wire are completely covered. Dry again and then sand smooth.

STEP 10

Fire the ring (the wire shank does not need to glow orange all around). Cool the ring slowly and then sand and burnish to a mirror finish. Burnishing the wire will stiffen it. Place the stone in the setting and secure.

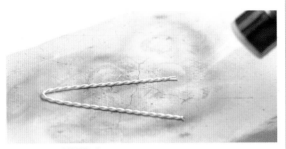

STEP 3

Bend the wire into a U-bend to make it a smaller mass and either heat it with a blowtorch until it glows pale red, or use a gas burner. This will make the wire soft and easy to shape around the mandrel. Cool by plunging in cold water.

STEP 4

Cut the wire in half and, with the two halves held together, wrap it around the mandrel at a point that is smaller than the required size to shape it into a circle. Now move it up to the correct point on the mandrel, over the prepared paper, and trim both pieces so that the wire is tight around the mandrel, with a gap at the top of 3mm.

Snake ring

Snake rings were popular with the ancient Greeks, who made them over 2,000 years ago. They have been copied by many cultures and are delightfully easy to make in metal clay. No join is required, and you can make the snake as elaborate or simple as you wish.

TOOLS & MATERIALS

- Basic toolkit
- 10g slow-dry silver metal clay
- Prepared ring mandrel with allowance for shrinkage (see page 75)
- Piece of string
- Small sheet of Perspex
- Modelling tool
- Tools for sanding, filing, brushing, polishing and burnishing
- Dark blue oil paint
- 1mm drill bit

STEP 1

Wrap a length of string twice around the paper on the mandrel and add 40mm. Cut off the string at this point.

STEP 2

Use a sheet of Perspex to roll out a 5mm thick log of clay and trim to the length of the piece of string. Point one end of the log for the tail; leave the other with a simple rounded end for the head.

STEP 3

Wet the log all along its length and apply the wetted side to the paper on the mandrel. Wind the log around the mandrel twice in the same way as you did with the string. Curl each end into an attractive shape so that they curve away from the main body of the ring.

STEP 4
Use a modelling tool to form a snake's snout. Use a needle to pierce two holes in the head for eyes, and two smaller holes at the end of the snout for nostrils. These can be refined at the plaster-dry stage. Brush over the coils with water as you work to keep them soft and prevent drying.

STEP 7
Use a drill bit to enlarge the eye holes.
Sand gently over the textured part, and sand the coils where they will pass under the palm side of the finger to thin them and make the ring more comfortable to wear.

STEP 10
When the ring is cool, brush, sand and polish. Use a burnisher to shine the textured areas and the crevices between the coils.

STEP 5
Use the eye of a large needle to impress scales all along the body of the snake. Start just behind the head and keep all the impressions in the same direction for realism.

STEP 8
Use a fine needle file to smooth inside the ring, but do not file away too much or the ring will be too big.

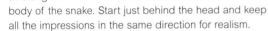

STEP 6
Dry the ring and remove from the paper (see steps 6–7, page 77). Sand any blemishes.

STEP 9
Fire the ring. If you use a gas burner, hang the head of the snake over the edge of the mesh so that the ring lies flat and place the mesh so that the whole of the ring on the edge of the mesh is in the red-hot area. Keep the head out of the direct flame or it may melt.

STEP 11
To accentuate the eyes, apply a tiny dab of oil paint and allow to dry. The ring lies comfortably on the finger when worn, with the head pointing towards the tip of the finger.

Filigree & Embellishments

Metal clay can be piped like icing from a syringe to create the delicate tracery of filigree jewellery. This chapter also shows how to embellish silver with pure gold, and how to simulate enamel and mother-of-pearl to enrich your jewellery projects with shimmering colour.

Making filigree

Silver metal clay is available in a semi-liquid form in a syringe so that it can be piped in delicate lines – in the same way as icing on a cake. This gives the opportunity for a gorgeous variety of filigree-type designs that require a fraction of the time to create compared to traditional filigree methods in silversmithing.

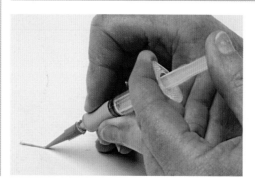

HOLDING THE SYRINGE

Hold the syringe in your non-working hand at an angle and use your working hand to guide the syringe. For the best control, press down the plunger with the thumb of your non-working hand. Always anchor the start and end of the line of filigree by dabbing down with the nozzle.

APPLICATION TYPES

Medium nozzle > line control:
For straight lines, always hold the syringe about 6mm above the surface and allow the line to fall into place, stretching it slightly as you extrude.

Medium nozzle > dots:
Hold the syringe almost upright, dab down and then draw upwards as you press the plunger to make dots of silver with pointed tops.

Medium nozzle > zigzag:
Dab down at each change of direction to anchor the line and make a zigzag.

Fine nozzle > random lines:
The fine nozzle is harder to control, so it is often used for random infill among the thicker lines of a medium or thick nozzle.

Fine nozzle > controlled lines:
Apply with the nozzle tip almost touching the surface. This controls the line but the result will be more irregular and thicker.

Thick nozzle > structural lines:
This gives a strong outline for pieces. Only two layers are needed with this nozzle to make the filigree strong enough.

FOLLOWING A DESIGN

STEP 1
Clean the tile thoroughly with alcohol and trace or draw the design onto it.

STEP 3
Continue around the piece until you have applied all of the lines of the design. If you make a mistake, you can scrape away bad lines and redraw. Use the wetted tip of a fine paintbrush to coax any minor errors into place.

STEP 5
Dry the piece completely. When cool, carefully free the piece from the tile with the tip of a knife and slip it off the tile.

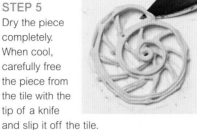

STEP 2
Syringe the inner lines of the design, turning the tile as you work. It is easier to pull the syringe towards you as you draw each line rather than push it.

STEP 4
Once the whole design has been drawn over, apply another line of syringe work over the top of the first. Apply a third layer over the outer lines of the design for strength. To make sure that the syringed lines remain crisp and do not sag before they dry, dry the syringe work lightly after applying each layer; a hair drier or heat gun is handy for this.

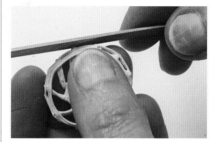

STEP 6
Gently file away any protruding spikes of clay. Be careful, because the piece is fragile and can snap if you apply too much pressure. Apply paste to any areas on the back that need reinforcing or smoothing. Dry again, then fire.

TIP
To prevent the clay in the syringe tip from drying out and forming a plug, always rest the tip of the syringe in water when not in use. Mop it dry and squeeze a little clay out into a paste pot before continuing, to make sure that the clay is flowing well. Always keep the syringe tip wiped clean of clay or water to prevent the line from curling over.

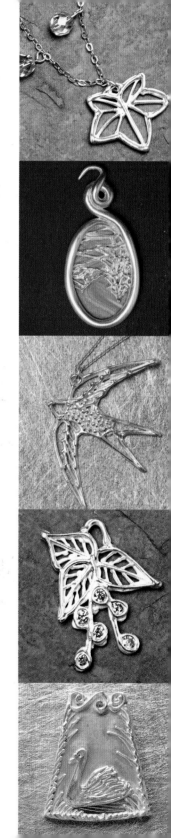

Feather earrings

Feathers are a lovely motif for jewellery. Natural objects are always easiest to create because they are so variable that the occasional wobble in your syringed lines will not look amiss.

TOOLS & MATERIALS

- Basic toolkit
- 10g syringe of silver metal clay with fine and medium nozzles
- Silver metal clay paste
- Template (see page 125)
- Tracing paper and pencil
- Alcohol
- Tools for filing, brushing and burnishing
- Two sterling silver earwires
- Round nose pliers

LEFT, FROM TOP:
- These delicate feather earrings show off the lines of silver filigree perfectly.
- This stained-glass effect pendant uses resin in several colours. Press the polished filigree onto a sheet of soft polymer clay and apply the resin. When it has set, remove the polymer clay backing.

STEP 1
Clean a tile with alcohol and trace the template onto it. If the traced pencil line is a bit faint, draw over it again freehand to darken the lines.

STEP 2
Use a medium nozzle to syringe the outlines of the design first, apply a single line of syringing for each stroke (see pages 84–85). Syringe a loop for hanging, making sure that it joins the outlines securely.

STEP 3

Now use a fine nozzle to syringe the inner lines of the design, applying two lines for each stroke. This is easier and quicker than going around the design twice. Start and end each stroke with a dab downwards to anchor it, and make sure that the inner lines all touch the outlines securely.

STEP 6

Apply clay down the central midrib of the feather and around the loop. This means that all lines have been applied twice. Finally, apply a third layer to the midrib and to the outlines as well if they need reinforcing. Repeat to make a second feather, tracing the back of the template onto another tile to reverse the image.

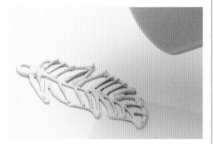

STEP 4

Part-dry the lines. This keeps the relief high and prevents the lines from flattening too much when additional lines are added.

STEP 7

Dry both feathers and carefully remove from the tiles.

STEP 9

Place the pieces back on a tile for support and brush over them carefully with a stainless steel brush. Brush along the lines of fine syringing, never across.

STEP 5

Use the medium nozzle to apply over all the outlines again, so that the ends of all the inner lines are covered neatly. Use a damp paintbrush to correct any mistakes by stroking the line back into place.

STEP 8

Apply paste to the back of the pieces to reinforce any fragile areas. File away any rough areas very gently – the pieces are very fragile. Fire and allow to cool.

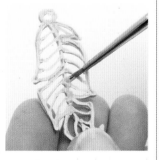

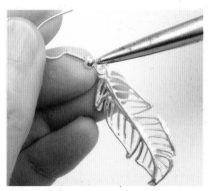

STEP 10

Burnish the pieces gently so as not to flatten the lines. Attach an earwire to each loop.

PROJECT 19 | Landscape pendant

Gossamer-fine lines of silver filigree are used to create a landscape pendant that is backed with marbled polymer clay for strength and colour. Once this technique is mastered, the possibilities are endless for making filigree pictures for jewellery.

ABOVE, FROM LEFT:
- Marbled lines of colour make a frosty sky behind the filigree mountains.
- Alter the colours of the polymer clay for a sunset pendant.
- Create close-up filigree landscapes, such as a lily pond with bulrushes.

STEP 1
Clean a tile with alcohol and trace the template onto it.

STEP 2
Using a fine nozzle, apply the lines of the mountains and water, applying two layers and then drying to keep the relief high. It is best to move the point quickly when using a fine syringe to stop the lines from syringing too fast and curling out of control.

STEP 3
Apply the lines of each fir tree by starting at the top of the tree and making a zigzag all the way down the tree on one side. Repeat on the other side of the tree and then fill in the centre with short lines.

STEP 6

Dry the piece and carefully remove it from the tile. Apply paste to the back of the piece to strengthen any areas that are not fully in contact with the log surround. Do not attempt to sand or file; the landscape is too fragile and any corrections can be made in the solid silver state. Fire the piece.

STEP 9

Lay the silver piece onto the marbled clay, aligning it to take best advantage of the swirls to suggest a frosty sky. Cut around the piece with a craft knife and remove the waste clay. Bake the piece on the tile as recommended on the polymer clay packet. The low curing temperature of the polymer clay will not harm the silver.

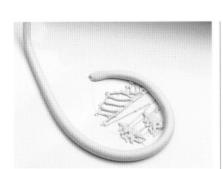

STEP 4

Roll a log of clay, 5mm thick and about 20cm long, using a sheet of Perspex if you find it hard to roll an even log. Point both ends of the log. Starting at the top of the piece, press one end of the log on the outline. Curve the log around the outline, making sure that it covers the edges of the landscape below.

STEP 7

When cool, lay the piece back on the tile for support and brush and burnish the silver filigree lines. A fine fibreglass brush is ideal for brushing delicate filigree. Sand the log frame to a mirror finish or leave it matt.

STEP 5

Make a loop in the log at the top and then curl the trailing edge into an attractive curve to finish. Apply paste where the log crosses over itself and use the syringe to apply infill if the log does not meet the landscape lines at any point.

STEP 8

Press together logs of each of the polymer clay colours and roll them together into a single log. Fold the log in half, then roll again. Repeat about 10 times until the log is marbled with fine streaks. Roll the log flat using a roller and 1mm rolling strips to give a swirling marbled sheet and place this on a tile.

STEP 10

When cool, remove the piece from the tile and attach a jump ring and chain. If the polymer clay does not seem secure, run some superglue between the silver and the polymer clay.

Jewelled filigree ring

The fluid lines of syringed filigree make beautiful rings. A filigree ring is very fragile in the plaster-dry state, so it has to be fired on the paper support. Once fired, however, it is remarkably strong. Refer also to the section on general ring techniques (see pages 74–75).

ABOVE, FROM LEFT:
- Gemstones add a wonderful sparkle to a filigree ring.
- Try freeform syringing, adding more loops and spirals in place of gemstones.

TOOLS & MATERIALS

- Basic toolkit
- 10g syringe of silver metal clay with medium nozzle
- Template (see page 125)
- Ring mandrel
- Sticky note
- Three 3mm fireable gemstones in colours of your choice
- Tools for brushing and burnishing

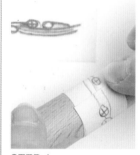

STEP 1
Trace the template onto the sticky note and then prepare the ring mandrel, allowing for clay shrinkage (see page 75).

STEP 2
To help you turn the mandrel as you syringe, place a box or pile of books about 10cm high on your work surface. Lay the prepared mandrel with the wide end on the books and the thin end on the work surface. Practise pushing the mandrel with your non-working hand so that you can operate the syringe with the other hand to apply lines of filigree in a continuous line around the mandrel.

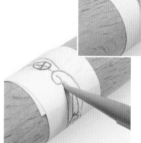

STEP 3
Anchor the syringed line with a dab on one of the guidelines on the paper and depress the syringe plunger to extrude a line of clay. Push the mandrel with your other hand to turn it slowly so that the syringed line drops onto the paper along the traced lines as you turn.

STEP 4

Continue around the mandrel, syringing lines over the traced design and creating spirals and loops where indicated. Create a base layer, then repeat to apply a second layer.

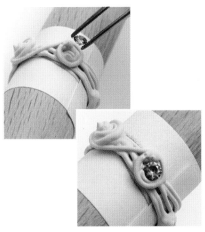

STEP 5

Use tweezers to place a gemstone in one of the loops indicated on the template.

STEP 6

Apply clay around the gemstone to hold it in place, making sure that the line covers the shoulder of the stone most of the way around. Repeat for the other two gemstones. Apply a third line of clay over any of the lines that need reinforcing or are too thin. Make sure that there are no gaps anywhere and that all lines are supported by at least one other.

STEP 7

Part-dry the ring and then carefully remove the ring on its paper support from the mandrel. Dry the ring fully, leaving it on the paper for firing because it will break if you try to remove it.

STEP 8

Fire the piece. If using a blowtorch, make sure that there are no flammable objects nearby; the paper will flare as it burns away, but will soon die down. Once the paper has burned away, leaving just ash, continue firing in the usual way for the required time. Cool the ring slowly.

STEP 9

Brush the ring carefully, supporting it from within. It is more likely to bend just after firing and will harden with burnishing. Avoid brushing over the stones and scratching them.

STEP 10

Burnish the ring along the lines to bring out the sparkle. Any sharp areas inside the ring should be filed away to give a smooth interior.

TIP

You will need to operate the syringe with one hand only for this project, because your non-working hand is needed to turn the mandrel. You may find it useful to practise applying filigree lines using one hand only on a flat surface first.

Embellishing with gold

Gold and silver look dazzling together. Gold metal clay is very expensive, so adding gold accents to silver metal clay is an economical way of using pure gold in your work.

GOLD LEAF

This technique is called 'keum-boo' and originated in the Far East. It is the method of applying gold leaf to another metal using heat to fuse the gold permanently onto the surface. Silver metal clay is a perfect surface for this, and you can use either a gas burner or a blowtorch.

STEP 3

Fire the piece on a gas burner or with a blowtorch until it glows pale orange, then switch off the flame. Holding the piece steady with tweezers, tap lightly all over the gold leaf with a burnisher to attach it to the silver below. Now burnish with a stroking action from the centre outwards to force out air bubbles and smooth down the gold.

TOOLS & MATERIALS

- Silver metal clay piece, newly fired but not brushed
- Gold leaf, preferably a thicker variety, such as the kind used for enamelling
- Superglue
- Tweezers
- Gas burner or blowtorch firing equipment
- Stainless steel tool for burnishing the gold; a spatula shape is good
- Agate burnisher
- Tools for brushing, sanding and polishing

STEP 1

Cut out the gold leaf in the required shape. This is easiest to do if you sandwich the leaf between two sheets of tracing paper, draw on the paper and cut out all together. You can also use paper punches to cut out a design.

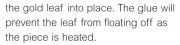

STEP 2

Apply a pin head of glue to the silver piece and use tweezers to lift the gold leaf into place. The glue will prevent the leaf from floating off as the piece is heated.

STEP 4

When cool, check that the gold leaf has adhered fully; if there are any loose parts, reheat the silver and repeat the process. Brush the silver area and then polish the gold with a microfine sanding pad or an agate burnisher.

GOLD PASTE

This process adds a painted layer of gold paste to fired (but not brushed or polished) silver. There are several gold paste products available. The technique varies slightly according to the product used, so be sure to read the instructions that come with the gold paste carefully. The following instructions use Art Clay Gold Paste. A gas burner is used to fire the gold paste here; the manufacturers of this brand do not recommend using a blowtorch. A kiln can be used instead.

TOOLS & MATERIALS

- Silver metal clay piece, fired but not brushed
- Gold paste
- Alcohol
- Paintbrush
- Gas burner or kiln firing equipment
- Tools for brushing and burnishing

STEP 1
Clean the piece with alcohol to remove any oil or dirt that may prevent the gold from adhering. If the piece is newly fired, this should not be necessary.

STEP 2
Stir the paste in the jar with a paintbrush. It should be the consistency of single cream. If it is too stiff to paint with, add a drop of water. Adding water will dilute the gold colour, so use the paste undiluted if possible. The bottle of medium that comes with the pot is used as a dilutent for painting on glass or porcelain only.

STEP 3
Paint the paste onto the silver in a layer about 0.5mm thick – half the thickness of a standard paperclip. Thicker paint may flake off. Allow the piece to dry naturally for about 15 minutes or put in an oven for 5 minutes at 150ºC. Paint on a second layer for a stronger gold colour and dry again.

STEP 4
Fire on a gas burner in the usual way, then turn off the burner and allow to cool. The gilded area should look a pale gold colour and matt. If there are white streaks in the gold area, the coating was too thin. Apply another coat of gold paste and refire.

STEP 5
Brush the silver and gold with a stainless steel brush, being gentle over the gold areas. Burnish with an agate or metal burnisher. If the gold is too pale, you can apply more gold paste, but refire the piece first to return it to the matt unpolished surface.

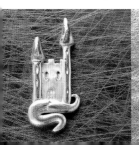

Rock art earrings

One of the delights of metal clay is that you can create fantastic textures. Here, granite has been impressed into the clay. The rough surface is then embellished with pure gold leaf, and the earrings are oxidized to create fabulous background colours.

LEFT, FROM TOP:
- The oxidation enhances the gold on the rock art earrings as well as colouring the silver.
- This variation features painted designs in gold paste instead of gold leaf cutouts.

TOOLS & MATERIALS

- Basic toolkit
- 10g silver metal clay
- Gold leaf, preferably a thicker variety, such as the kind used for enamelling
- Template (see page 125)
- Piece of stone or rock with a granular texture
- Paper punch with a simple motif
- Baking parchment
- Superglue
- 1mm drill bit
- Tools for filing, brushing, sanding and burnishing
- Liver of sulphur
- Silver earwires
- Round nose pliers

STEP 1

Roll out a 1mm thick sheet of metal clay and lay it onto a rock. Press all over the back of the clay to impress the rough texture onto the clay sheet.

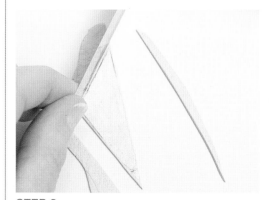

STEP 2

Lay the template over the clay sheet and cut around it, then reverse the template to cut out a second piece for a matching pair of earrings.

STEP 3

Use a file to roughen the edges of the triangles

to suggest hewn rock. Make a hole in the top of each earring and dry the pieces thoroughly. When dry, redrill the holes with a drill bit. File smooth any rough edges, but leave them with a good rocky texture. Fire and leave unbrushed in the white state.

STEP 4

Sandwich the gold leaf in a folded sheet of baking parchment. With the punch upside down so that you can see where you are punching, slide the leaf in its wrapping into the slot of the punch until you can see that the hole is filled with the leaf and paper. Press down firmly onto the punch and remove the cutout pieces, discarding the baking parchment. Repeat for the second motif.

STEP 5

Attach a gold leaf piece to each fired earring with a little superglue to hold it in place, then fire (see page 92).

STEP 6

Brush over each piece with a stainless steel brush, taking care to be gentle over the gold leaf. Burnish the gold leaf with a burnisher or use a microfine sanding pad to bring out the shine.

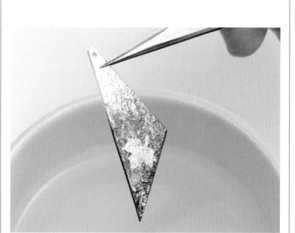

STEP 7

Oxidize each piece with liver of sulphur. To get a variegated colour, dip only the bottom of the piece first, then when the colour begins to change, dip deeper by degrees so that the bottom has much longer in the solution than the top. Remove when the colour is blue at the bottom, grading to orange and silver at the top.

STEP 8

Rinse thoroughly. The oxidation is on a textured surface, so it should not rub off with time. Attach the earwires to the tops of the earrings.

IMPRESSED LEAVES

Use the paper punch to cut out leaf shapes from card stock. Roll these onto a sheet of untextured clay to impress the leaves into the clay. Remove the cutouts to reveal the indented design. Embellish with a gold leaf cutout, then oxidize.

Gilded castle pendant

This fairytale castle is made using simple sculpting techniques and is then embellished with gold paste. The piece could also be made as a brooch; see page 49 for how to attach a brooch finding to the back.

TOOLS & MATERIALS

- Basic toolkit
- 10g slow-dry silver metal clay
- Silver metal clay paste
- Gold paste
- Templates (see page 125)
- Clear plastic and ballpoint pen or permanent marker
- Miniature chisel tool made by hammering the end of a paperclip flat
- Pencil and engraving tool
- Tools for sanding, brushing and burnishing
- Two pure silver screw eyes
- Sterling silver chain
- Two sterling silver jump rings
- Wire cutters and round nose pliers

LEFT, FROM TOP:
- Use gold paste to highlight key areas of the design, such as windows, turrets and battlements.
- Vary the arrangement of turrets and keep. Smaller castles make stylish tie tacks.

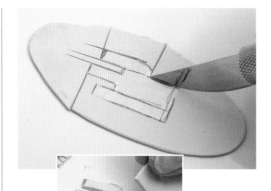

STEP 1

Roll out a 1mm thick sheet of silver metal clay and place on a tile. Trace both templates onto clear plastic. Lay the larger template onto the clay and cut out the keep and towers. Remove the waste clay. The castle should not be moved until it has been dried.

STEP 2

Mark lines on the castle where indicated, using the side of a darning needle to emphasize the keep and towers.

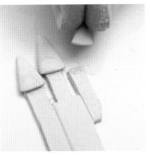

STEP 3
Form a 10mm ball of clay and shape it into a teardrop with a sharp point. Flatten onto the tile and cut off the bottom to make a turret roof, about 13mm long. Repeat to make two more roofs. Apply paste to the top of each tower and press on a roof so that the bottom of the roof overlaps the tower slightly.

STEP 4
Brush water over the castle to keep it moist.

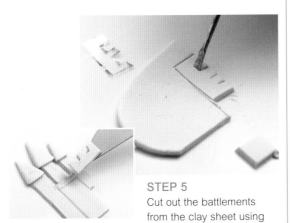

STEP 5
Cut out the battlements from the clay sheet using the smaller template and use a chisel tool to remove the clay from between the crenellations. Apply paste to the top of the castle keep and press on the battlements.

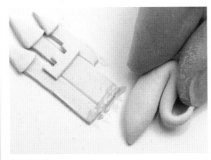

STEP 6
Form a 13mm ball of clay and shape it into a 40mm long log with pointed ends. Taper the right-hand end more than the other. Apply paste to the base of the castle and press on the log, curling the tapered end around into an attractive swirl.

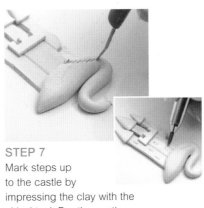

STEP 7
Mark steps up to the castle by impressing the clay with the chisel tool. Dry the castle thoroughly on the tile. Sand the surface to smooth any rough areas and sand the back as well. Mark windows and door with a pencil, and then use an engraving tool to engrave them.

STEP 8
Use paste to attach the screw eyes to the back of the castle, making sure that they are level. Apply paste to the joins at the backs of the turrets to strengthen them. Dry again and then sand away excess paste to make the back neat.

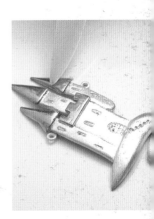

STEP 9
Fire the piece. Apply two coats of gold paste to the turret roofs, the windows and the door. Fire again (see page 93). When cool, brush the silver and leave it matt. Burnish the gold areas.

STEP 10
Cut the chain in half and use jump rings to attach each end to a screw eye.

Embellishing with resin

Two-part epoxy resin is a superb way of producing deep pools of glassy enamel effects on metal clay. While true enamel can discolour on silver, resin can be used to produce virtually any colour. It also requires no special equipment, such as a kiln. Resin can also be used as a protective coating over fragile materials, such as mother-of-pearl mosaic.

TOOLS & MATERIALS

- Basic toolkit
- 10g silver metal clay
- Paper punch with a tiny motif and card stock
- Oval cutter
- Tools for brushing, sanding and polishing
- Two-part clear coating epoxy resin
- Two syringes
- Mixing cup and spatula
- Alcohol
- Oil paints in colours of your choice – alizarin crimson, cobalt blue and zinc yellow are used here to make a rainbow of colour

RESIN AS FAUX ENAMEL

This example uses motifs cut out in card stock with a paper punch to make cavities in the clay, which are then filled with coloured resin.

STEP 1

Use a paper punch to cut out a shape from card stock. Roll out a 1mm thick sheet of clay and lay the shape onto it. Roll again between the rolling strips to impress the card into the clay. Remove the card shape.

STEP 2

Position a cutter over the impressed  shape and cut out the pendant. Use a needle to make a hole at one end, then dry, sand and fire. Brush and polish the pendant to a mirror finish.

STEP 3

Measure the resin and hardener into the mixing cup according to the instructions on the pack. Resin is usually mixed 1 part resin to 1 part hardener. Use separate syringes for  resin and hardener and keep them labelled for future use. Mix up about ½ tsp; this will be plenty for most small jewellery items.

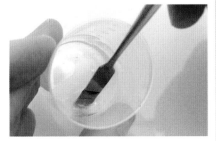

STEP 4

Use a spatula to mix the resin for at least 1 minute or as advised on the pack. Take care to scrape resin off the sides and mix it in. Bubbles will develop as you mix, but these should disperse when the mixture is left to stand for a few minutes.

STEP 5

Scoop out some resin onto a tile. Add a pin head of crimson oil paint and use the spatula to mix the colour into the resin, flattening any lumps of colour.

STEP 6

Soak a cotton bud in alcohol and clean the silver to degrease it. Scoop up a little coloured resin on the end of a blunt tapestry needle and apply it to the impressed cavity. Push the resin into the corners and edges with the point of the needle.

STEP 7

Mix yellow oil paint into another pool of resin and apply to the silver just beyond the first colour. Use a fine needle to drag the colours into each other for graded effects. The crimson and yellow will make an orange colour where they mix.

STEP 8

Mix blue paint into a third pool of resin and apply as before, dragging it towards the yellow resin to mix and make green between the two. Set the piece aside and cover with an upturned glass or box to prevent dust from settling on the resin surface before it has hardened. Most resins will cure to a solid state overnight, but check the pack. The set resin is durable and permanent. The glassy surface is extremely hard, but can be filed or sanded and then polished if necessary.

TIPS

- Use a clear coating resin rather than an embedding resin. The former is thicker and can be domed for a pleasing effect. It will also cling in a thicker coat to a surface that is not entirely level. Embedding resin is more liquid and harder to control.
- Work in a dust-free atmosphere to avoid dust landing on the resin surface before it is set and spoiling it.
- Work in a warm room and leave the resin to set in a warm place for quicker setting.
- Some resins are supplied with colours, but you can achieve excellent results using good-quality oil paint as pigment, which gives a huge palette of colours.
- Clean up with alcohol and avoid touching the liquid resin with your fingers – in rare cases, it can cause an allergic reaction.

Pinewoods bracelet

Tiny rubber stamps are used to impress the links of this pretty bracelet, which are then embellished with pools of resin to simulate glassy enamel. You can use any stamps you like for the impressions, but make sure that they are small and detailed.

TOOLS & MATERIALS

- Basic toolkit
- 25g silver metal clay
- Small, detailed rubber stamps, such as a pinecone and fir tree branch
- Vegetable oil
- 20mm square cutter
- 1mm drill bit
- Tools for brushing, sanding, polishing and burnishing
- Two-part clear coating epoxy resin
- Two syringes
- Mixing cup and spatula
- Oil paints – ultramarine blue, viridian, yellow and violet
- 4mm sterling silver jump rings; you will need 45 for an eight-link bracelet
- Silver lobster clasp and 25mm length of sterling silver chain
- Round nose pliers

LEFT:
- The bracelet is 20cm long; adjust the length by adding or subtracting links.
- A sea-themed variation.

STEP 1

Roll out a 1mm thick sheet of clay, about 5cm wide and several inches long. Place on a tile. Rub the stamps in a little vegetable oil and impress the clay with the stamps in a line all along the strip. Angle the stamps in different directions and overlap the impressions to build up an image of pinecones in a fir tree.

STEP 2

Use a square cutter to cut out eight links, positioning the cutter so that at least part of each square will have an area of smooth silver.

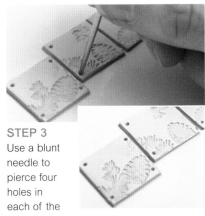

STEP 3

Use a blunt
needle to
pierce four
holes in
each of the
first seven links, about 2mm in from the
corners and at the same position on each
so that they will all line up. Cut one of the
squares into a triangle for the end link and
make three holes in this.

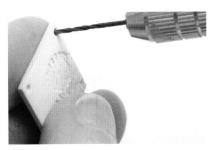

STEP 4

Dry all the links thoroughly, then
sand smooth. Drill the holes again
with a drill bit.

STEP 5

Fire the pieces. You can fire several at a time on
a gas burner, provided that all the pieces are in the
glowing red area of the mesh. When cool, brush,
sand and polish the links. Leave the back with a
brushed satin finish. Burnish the edges of each link,
then clean the surface of the links with alcohol to
degrease them.

STEP 6

Mix up ½ tsp of resin
(see page 99). Mix the
resin on a tile with viridian
oil paint to make a fir
green. Add a little yellow
to make a warmer green,
and touches of blue
and violet to make
a darker green.

STEP 7

Use a tapestry or wool
needle to apply pools
of the fir green to the
stamped fir branches,
filling the cavities. Try not
to overfill, so that the resin
does not flow over the
unstamped areas. Apply
yellow and darker greens
to vary the colours.

STEP 8

Mix violet and blue paint into more
resin for the pinecones. Apply to the
cone stampings, and add some clear
resin to one side of each cone to
suggest a highlight.

STEP 9

Join the links with
three jump rings
on each hole, so
that the links will
lie flat on the wrist.
Attach the clasp to the triangle with a
single jump ring, and the chain to the
other end link with two jump rings.

Mother-of-pearl fan

Mother-of-pearl inlay is an ancient Japanese craft, and what better design to show it off than a traditional Japanese fan? The technique is not difficult, but you need a steady hand to place the tiny mosaic pieces of mother of pearl.

ABOVE:
An inlaid Japanese fan makes a stylish pendant.

BELOW:
A variation embellished with maple leaves instead of flowers.

TOOLS & MATERIALS

- Basic toolkit
- 10g silver metal clay
- Silver metal clay paste
- Templates (see page 125)
- Tracing paper, pencil and card stock
- Clear plastic and ballpoint pen or permanent marker
- 5mm flower cutter
- Tools for sanding, brushing and polishing
- Alcohol
- Black acrylic paint
- Mother-of-pearl sheet
- Rubber block or cutting mat
- Clear gloss varnish
- Two-part clear coating epoxy resin
- Two syringes
- Mixing cup and spatula
- Small pure silver screw eye
- Silver chain and jump ring
- Round nose pliers

STEP 1
Trace the river template onto card stock and cut out. Roll out a 1mm thick sheet of clay and place on a tile. Lay the cutout onto the clay and roll the clay again to impress the river onto the clay surface. Remove the card carefully.

STEP 3
Roll a log, 3mm thick and 25mm long, pointed at one end. Roll the centre with the handle of a paintbrush to groove it in two places, and then flatten the rounded end.

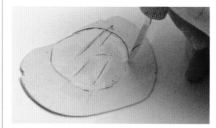

STEP 2
Trace the fan template onto plastic and cut out. Lay it onto the clay, aligning the river lines, and cut around it. Remove the waste clay from around the fan.

STEP 4
Apply paste to the base of the fan head and press on the handle, pushing it well down to secure.

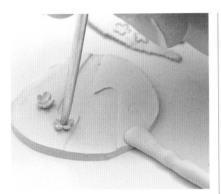

STEP 5
Roll out a thin sheet of clay two playing cards thick and cut out five flowers with a cutter. Press a blunt needle onto each petal to cup it, then use paste to attach the flowers to the fan. Attach a screw eye to the top back of the fan with paste. Dry, sand and then fire. When cool, brush all over and burnish the flowers.

STEP 6
Brush the area of the river with alcohol to degrease. Colour it with black paint and allow to dry.

STEP 7
Lay the mother-of-pearl sheet on a rubber block or mat and wet with water to stop the pieces from flying off when cut. Use a craft knife to cut 2mm wide strips from the sheet, and then cut these into triangles. To cut, press the knife blade down onto the sheet and it will fracture along the line of the blade.

STEP 8
Let the pieces dry. Apply a dab of varnish to a small area of the black paint and then use the sticky tip of the brush to pick up and apply a triangle of mother of pearl. Push it into place while the varnish is still wet. Repeat to apply a row along the edge of the black area.

STEP 9
Continue applying the triangles, using the varnish to attach them, aligning one side of the triangles along the edges of the river. Then work inwards from the edges, applying the triangles in a regular pattern and cutting any smaller pieces needed to fill the area. Leave a tiny space between the triangles so that the black shows as thin lines.

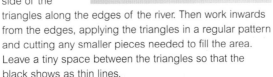

STEP 10
Varnish over the whole area to consolidate the pieces and allow to dry thoroughly. Mix up the resin (see page 99) and leave for 5–10 minutes for the bubbles to disperse and the mixture to thicken a little. Apply the resin over the mosaic area, doming it slightly, but do not let it creep beyond the edges of the river.

STEP 11
Cover with an upturned glass or cup and leave overnight in a warm place for the resin to set. The resin will act like a lens and enhance the mosaic colours. Attach a chain with a jump ring.

Using a Kiln

A small jewellery kiln is a wonderful investment, and modern technology has made kilns safe and easy to use. This chapter covers some of the enticing techniques that require a kiln, including glorious dichroic glass and delicate paper clay projects.

Fused glass cabochons

The newer low-fire kinds of metal clay are ideal for firing with glass embellishments, such as dichroic glass cabochons. Creating fused glass cabochons is not difficult with a small programmable kiln.

FORMING THE CABOCHON

The simplest kind of cabochon is made from two pieces of glass: dichroic-coated black glass on the bottom and clear glass on the top. Heated in a kiln, the two pieces fuse together into a rounded cabochon.

STEP 1

Cut a 15 x 20mm rectangle of dichroic glass. To cut the glass, lay a ruler or straight edge on the back of the glass at the point where you want to cut. Use a glass cutter or engraving tool to score a fine line.

STEP 2

Hold the glass in a pair of breaking pliers about 6mm from the edge, with the centre of the pliers positioned over the score line. The shaped breaking pliers should always have their convex side upwards. Squeeze gently and the glass will snap along the scored line. Repeat to complete the rectangle.

STEP 3

Cut another rectangle of clear glass, but make it about 2mm larger all around than the dichroic glass. Use a felt-tipped pen to mark the cutting line.

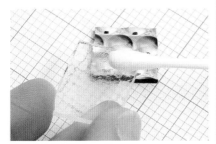

STEP 4

Clean all the surfaces of the glass pieces with a cotton bud dipped in alcohol. Apply a tiny quantity of PVA glue or superglue to the coloured dichroic glass and press on the clear glass, positioning it carefully so that it is centred. The glue will hold the two pieces temporarily together until they are safely in the kiln.

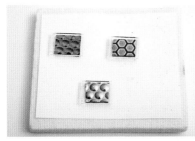

STEP 5

Repeat to cut more glass pieces and assemble in the same way. Lay all the pieces on a ceramic paper-covered firing board and place in a cold kiln.

FUSING THE GLASS

Note that these instructions only apply to kilns with a chamber size of about 20cm cubed or smaller. Larger kilns will need lower firing temperatures because they take longer to heat up, so you should refer to the kiln instructions.

STEP 1

Switch on the kiln and set it to heat to 870ºC at full speed. When the temperature is reached, hold it at that temperature for about 5 minutes. Open the kiln door and check the glass. The glass will slowly become more rounded as you hold the temperature; 10 minutes is usually about right with a small kiln.

STEP 2

Switch off the kiln, but leave the temperature display on. Hold the kiln door open about 7.5cm and let the temperature drop to 550ºC. Shut the door immediately and allow the kiln to reach room temperature.

STEP 3

Remove the glass from the kiln and rinse to remove any powder from the shelf paper. The pieces are now ready to mount.

SAFETY

Always wear safety goggles when cutting glass – a shard of glass in the eye can cause blindness. Work over newspaper and take care of glass splinters, which are inevitable when cutting glass. When you have finished working, gather up the newspaper with any shards in it, wrap up carefully and dispose.

TIPS

- Proper glass-cutting tools make accurate cutting much easier. However, if you are just experimenting, you can improvise with an engraving tool to score the glass and ordinary pliers to snap it.
- It is important to use dichroic glass of the same coefficient of expansion (COE) to avoid cracking. COE 90 glass is widely available from dichroic glass suppliers.

| **Icicle pendant**

Spiky slivers of silver mimic icicles encasing a glass cabochon. The technique of firing the metal clay on the glass and allowing the glass to soften again slightly results in the metal clay grabbing the glass securely as it shrinks onto the softened glass.

TOOLS & MATERIALS

- Basic toolkit
- 7g silver metal clay; slow-dry clay is easiest
- Silver metal clay paste
- Small piece of 1.5mm thick patterned dichroic clear glass (COE 90)
- Small piece of 1.5mm thick white glass (COE 90)
- Glass-cutting and breaking tools (see pages 106–107)
- 13mm circle cutter
- Tissue blade
- Tools for sanding, filing, brushing and burnishing
- Sterling silver chain

LEFT, FROM TOP:
- Dichroic clear glass is perfect for an icy look.
- A cutout flower of metal clay is used as the mount for a blue glass cabochon.
- Apply a clay circle as a mount; drag a blunt needle through it to add texture.

STEP 1

To make a triangular-shaped glass cabochon, cut the white glass into a long triangle about 40mm long and 15mm wide at the top. Cut the clear dichroic glass in the same shape, but about 2mm wider all around. Place the dichroic glass, pattern side down, over the white glass and fuse (see pages 106–107).

STEP 2

Roll out a 1mm thick sheet of clay and cut out a circle with a cutter. Press this onto the top of the cabochon.

STEP 3

Cut a 5 x 25mm strip of clay from the sheet. Lay it on a tile and place a thick tapestry needle across the centre of the strip. Apply paste to the bottom end. Pull the strip over the needle and press down onto the pasted clay to secure and make a loop. Trim the bottom to about 13mm long.

STEP 4

Apply paste to the protruding strip of the loop and press the cabochon onto it so that the back of the applied circle mount is attached firmly to the loop. Do not remove the needle or the piece from the tile until the clay is dry.

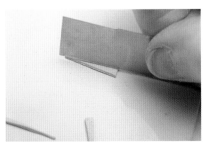

STEP 5

Use a tissue blade to cut long pointed strips of clay from the clay sheet in a variety of lengths.

STEP 6

Apply paste to the front of the circle mount and press the strips onto it in an attractive arrangement. Vary the lengths of the pointed strips to suggest a scattering of icicles. Cut the tops of some of the strips into a point to insert between the others and so cover the circle mount.

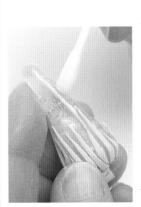

STEP 7

Dry the piece, then carefully file or sand away any irregularities on the loop. Take care when sanding the icicles, which will be very fragile. Use a damp cotton bud to remove any smears of silver clay from the glass.

STEP 8

Fire in the same way as when fusing the glass cabochon, but this time set the temperature to reach 800ºC and hold for 5 minutes before cooling.

STEP 9

Remove the piece from the kiln and wipe away any powder from the shelf paper. Brush over the silver and then burnish to a shine. Take care not to lever against the silver or it may crack the glass. Thread a chain through the loop.

TIP

Timings and temperatures are for a small kiln with a chamber 20cm cubed or less. For a larger kiln, refer to the anufacturer's instructions because the temperature requirements will be lower.

Paper clay techniques

Metal clay comes in various forms and one of the most intriguing is the type called either paper or sheet clay, depending on the brand. Both have similar properties and can be used for all kinds of projects that are based on techniques such as paper cutting, paper folding and quilling.

TYPES OF PAPER CLAY

The two brands available are different in thickness and quality. Art Clay Paper Type on the left is thicker and more like thin card than PMC Sheet, which behaves more like fabric. For ease of reference, the product is referred to as paper clay here.

STORAGE TIPS

Store paper clay in its original envelope in a resealable plastic bag and keep away from heat. Use the packet up reasonably quickly after opening; it is softest and easiest to work when new. If the sheet cracks when you fold it, it is old stock; use this for paper punch embellishments.

TOOLS & MATERIALS

- Basic toolkit
- Silver metal paper clay
- Ordinary silver metal clay
- Silver metal clay paste
- Paper punch, texturing material and cutter
- Sharp scissors
- Tracing paper and pencil
- Tools for brushing, sanding and burnishing

PAPER PUNCH EMBELLISHMENTS

STEP 1
Use a paper punch upside down so that you can see where you are placing the paper clay in the punch. When it fills the area of the shape, press down.

STEP 2
Roll out a sheet of ordinary metal clay and texture it with fabric, a leaf or a detailed texture sheet. Cut out the required shape and pierce or add a finding.

CUTTING AND FOLDING

Paper clay is rather like thin leather and can be folded easily. Folding strengthens the thin sheet. Art Clay Paper Type is the easiest to use for this technique, because it has more rigidity.

STEP 3
Paint the back of the paper clay motif with paste and press it onto the textured clay. The motif will be fragile, so take care not to break off any projecting parts. Dry thoroughly, then sand and fire in a kiln (see Finishing Tips). Brush the piece, taking care around the paper clay motif. Use a microfine sanding pad to polish the motif and burnish the textured area behind it.

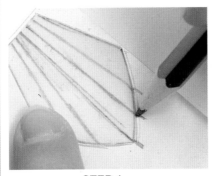

STEP 1
Make a template for the required shape and place it onto the clay sheet. Draw on the fold lines.

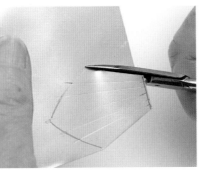

STEP 2
Cut out the shape with sharp scissors.

STEP 3
Lay a straight edge on top of the clay, along the line to be folded, and use a straight blade to press the sheet upwards to crease it accurately along the line.

STEP 4
Run a fingertip along the folded edge to crease it firmly. Flip the sheet to make a fold in the other direction.

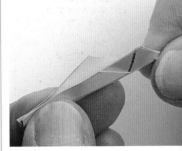

STEP 5
When the whole piece is creased, fold it up as shown to accentuate the fold lines.

GENERAL TIPS

- Create the piece first in paper and then use that as a pattern or template for the paper clay.
- Paper clay does not dry out, so take your time over elaborate projects.
- You need to work completely dry – DO NOT add water while you work. If paper clay gets too damp, it may start to distintegrate.
- Paper clay combines happily with other forms of silver metal clay; just take care not to get it too wet when using paste to glue it to other kinds.
- Because it is so thin, paper clay can produce quite fragile jewellery. Either use it as embellishments for other clay projects, or put folds or coils into the paper clay design to add strength.

FINISHING TIPS

- Pure silver findings can be added in the usual way with clay paste before firing. Fire soon after applying the paste or the paper clay may begin to disintegrate with the moisture.
- Alternatively, add findings with oil paste after firing, which may be preferable because it avoids the problem of the paper clay becoming too wet.
- There is no need to dry the paper clay before firing unless there are other kinds of clay in the piece. If you have two kinds of clay, fire for the kind requiring the hottest and longest firing.
- Brush, sand and polish fired pieces carefully; they can bend if you press too hard. Support each part while you work, because it is easy to crack the clay.
- Any cracks or problem areas can be repaired or reinforced with oil paste and then fired again.

Fan and flower earrings

The concertina folding of these pretty earrings gives the paper-thin silver added strength. The same basic design can be used to make a pair of small fan earrings with pearl drops, or adapted to create flower earrings with colourful beads.

TOOLS & MATERIALS

- Basic toolkit
- 5g silver metal paper clay; Art Clay is easiest to use for this project
- Silver metal clay paste
- Template (see page 125)
- Tracing paper and pencil
- Sharp scissors
- Tissue blade
- Tools for brushing, sanding and polishing
- Two pure silver screw eyes
- Four 40mm long sterling silver headpins
- Four small pearl beads; two of each colour
- Two 4mm sterling silver jump rings
- Two sterling silver earwires
- Wire cutters and round nose pliers

LEFT, FROM TOP:
- Glossy pearls look beautiful with silver clay fans.
- Adapt the fan to make delicate harebell flower earrings and team with brightly coloured beads.

FAN EARRINGS

STEP 1

Trace the fan template onto the paper clay and cut out two pieces. Use a ruler or straight edge to fold the lines on the pattern (see page 111). It is easier to crease all the folds first and then reform them to shape the pieces.

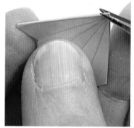

STEP 2

Cut a notch in the centre top and use paste to attach a screw eye on the top back of each piece. Allow to dry for about 20 minutes in a warm place. Do not use a hair drier or artificial heat because this may crack the paper clay. Alternatively, attach the screw eyes with oil paste after firing. Prop the pieces with fibre cloth to prevent the folds from sagging, then fire in a kiln.

STEP 3

Bend the pieces gently back into shape if they have flattened during firing. Brush gently, sand with a microfine sanding pad and polish, supporting the pieces well from below. Alternatively, you can burnish, but this will leave lines in the silver.

STEP 4

Thread a bead onto each headpin and trim two of the headpins by about 3mm. Turn a loop in the top of each headpin (see page 59) and attach two headpins to each jump ring.

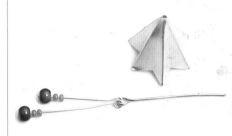

STEP 5

Attach the loop on each earwire to the screw eye on the fan and add one of the jump rings so that the beads hang behind the fan.

TOOLS & MATERIALS

- Basic toolkit
- 5g silver metal paper clay
- Silver metal clay paste
- Template (see page 125)
- Tracing paper and pencil
- Sharp scissors
- Tissue blade
- Tools for brushing, sanding and polishing
- Four 50mm long sterling silver headpins
- Two 25mm lengths of 0.8mm silver wire
- Four 5mm purple beads
- Eight fuchsia seed beads
- Two 3mm frosted white beads
- Two sterling silver earwires
- Wire cutters and round nose pliers

FLOWER EARRINGS

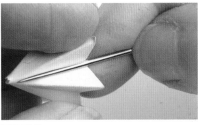

STEP 1

Trace the flower template onto the paper clay and cut out two pieces. Fold in the same way as the fan earrings, then shape the fan into a cone and use paste to join the ends, overlapping them.

STEP 3

If the folds flatten during firing, accentuate them by pressing the side of a needle into the folds. Brush gently, sand with a microfine sanding pad and polish; support the pieces well from the inside when working on the outside.

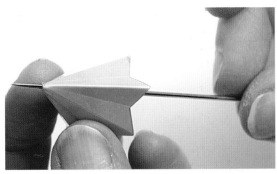

STEP 2

Push a needle through the top to make sure that there is a hole. Place the flowers upright on a firing board and fire, supporting them with fibre cloth to prevent sagging.

STEP 4

For each flower, thread a purple bead and two seed beads onto each of two headpins; shorten one by trimming off about 6mm. Turn a loop in the top of each headpin (see page 59). Form a loop at one end of a piece of wire and attach the headpin loops. Pull the wire through the flower so the loop is inside. Thread on a frosted bead, trim to 6mm and make a loop. Attach an earwire to the top loop.

Quilled leaf pendant

Quilling is a Victorian papercraft technique of rolling up strips of paper into coils that are then glued together into bigger units. Paper clay can be rolled up in a similar way and glued with paste before firing.

TOOLS & MATERIALS

- Silver metal paper clay – this project uses Art Clay Silver Paper Type, which measures 75mm square; if you use PMC+ Sheet, cut the strips into 75mm lengths
- Silver metal clay paste
- Graph paper and pencil
- Cocktail stick
- Tools for brushing and burnishing
- Large sterling silver jump ring
- Leather thong or sterling silver chain
- Round nose pliers

LEFT, FROM TOP:
- Quilling is ideal for natural designs, such as a leaf.
- Flower earrings made from six almond-shaped coils.
- Two strips have been joined together to make large almond coils for the upper wings of this butterfly variation. The antennae are short strips coiled at one end.

STEP 1
Lay the paper clay over a sheet of graph paper and mark the edges in increments of 3mm.

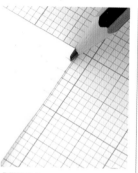

STEP 2
Using a ruler or straight edge and a sharp knife, cut 3 x 75mm strips using the whole width of the sheet.

STEP 3
Lay a cocktail stick on the end of a strip and roll the strip tightly around the stick. Keep the coil straight and as tight as possible.

STEP 4

Remove the coil from the stick and place on the work surface to allow it to relax a little and form a looser coil. To prevent it from opening too much, lay rolling strips on either side of it about 10mm apart.

STEP 5

Place a dab of paste just under the end of the strip and press it down. Allow to dry for about 3 minutes.

STEP 6

You can now leave the coil as a circle or pinch it into a variety of shapes. To make an almond shape, for example, hold the coil in both hands and pinch with the thumb and forefinger of each hand.

STEP 7

For a teardrop, pinch one side only into a point. To make a semicircle, pinch at two points a third of the way around the coil from each other. It is safest to pinch the coils so that the join is in a flat area between the points. For the pendant, make two almond shapes, one long thin almond shape (pinch it harder) and two semicircles. You will also need half a strip made into a circle for the top loop.

TIP

Quilling with paper clay produces beautiful but rather fragile results, so this technique is best used for pendants and drop earrings only. To make brooches, back the coils with a sheet of silver or polymer clay for extra strength.

STEP 8

Assemble the pieces into a leaf design, with the circle at the top, two semicircles next, then two almond shapes and finally the long thin almond shape as the point at the bottom. Make sure that they touch each other on all sides for strength, and use dabs of paste to glue the coils to each other. Cut a strip of paper clay and paste it on the centre of the piece where all the coils join to reinforce it (this side will be the back of the pendant).

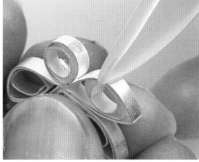

STEP 9

Allow to dry in a warm place for about 15 minutes. Place in a cool kiln on a firing board and fire. Remove from the kiln and allow to cool slowly. Brush very gently and then burnish all the sides of the coils and the top.

STEP 10

Attach a jump ring to the top coil. Thread through a leather thong or silver chain.

Gallery

Metal clay has a relatively short history, but already its influence on the jewellery and craft worlds has been far-reaching. Here is a selection of pieces from talented artists around the world who work with this glorious material.

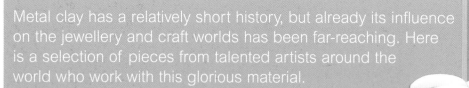

MARIKO KONNO
Start
Left: An intricate silver metal clay watchband decorated with beautifully sculpted miniature turtles and seashells. Syringed filigree adds texture to the background.

REBECCA SKEELS
Spotty Crow
Left: A silver metal clay ring in the whimsical design of a stylized crow. The ring is displayed on stainless steel legs that double as a stand.

CINDY GARD-KOIZUMI
Engraved Garnet Ring
Above: A simple and stylish ring with delicate engraving set with an embedded garnet.

YUKIKO KUDO
Fantasy
Left: Every detail on this three ring set demonstrates exquisite miniature sculpture. Embedded crystals, gemstones and moulding as well as bas-relief on the shanks create a fabulous effect.

MAKI KINOSHITA
Beyond the River (Go for It!)
Below: A delightfully lively and humorous design, the naive-style picture on the flat table of the ring adds to the charm.

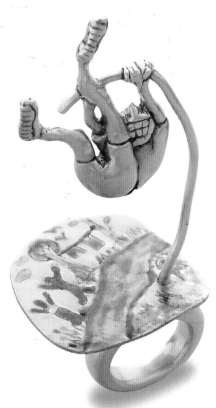

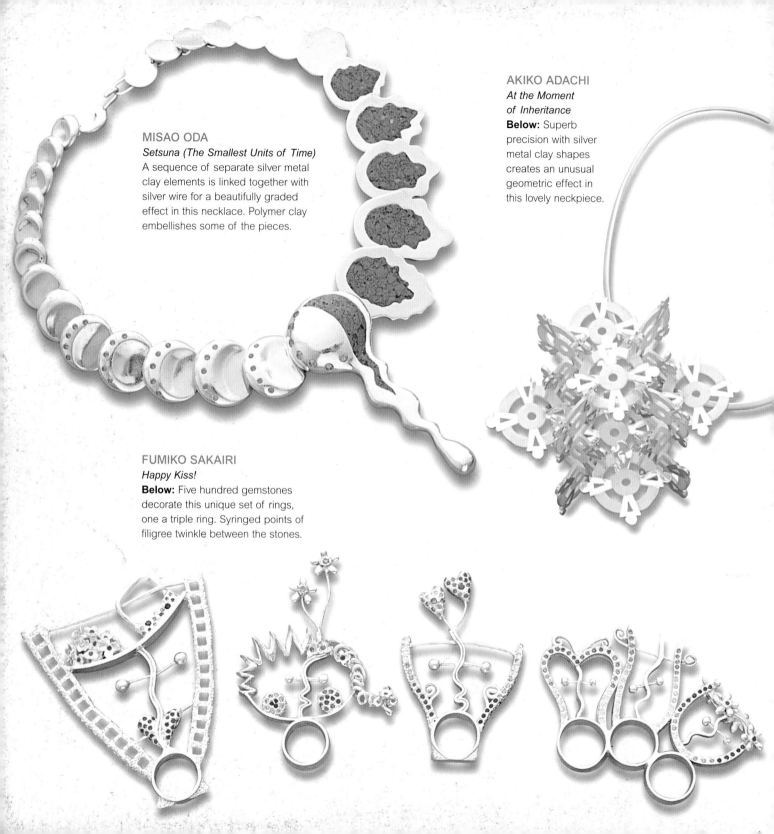

MISAO ODA
Setsuna (The Smallest Units of Time)
A sequence of separate silver metal clay elements is linked together with silver wire for a beautifully graded effect in this necklace. Polymer clay embellishes some of the pieces.

AKIKO ADACHI
At the Moment of Inheritance
Below: Superb precision with silver metal clay shapes creates an unusual geometric effect in this lovely neckpiece.

FUMIKO SAKAIRI
Happy Kiss!
Below: Five hundred gemstones decorate this unique set of rings, one a triple ring. Syringed points of filigree twinkle between the stones.

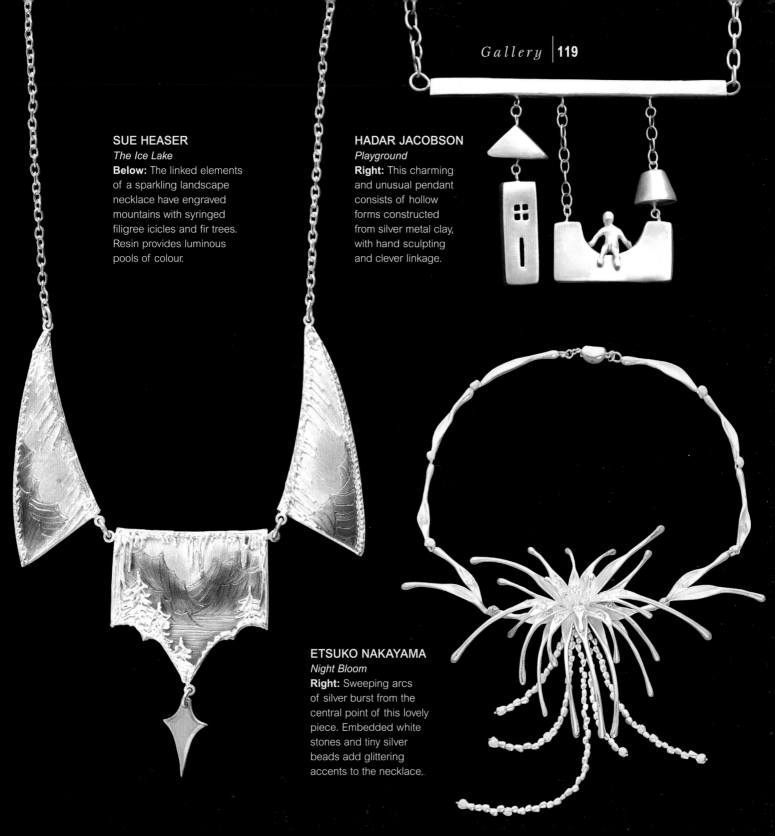

SUE HEASER
The Ice Lake
Below: The linked elements of a sparkling landscape necklace have engraved mountains with syringed filigree icicles and fir trees. Resin provides luminous pools of colour.

HADAR JACOBSON
Playground
Right: This charming and unusual pendant consists of hollow forms constructed from silver metal clay, with hand sculpting and clever linkage.

ETSUKO NAKAYAMA
Night Bloom
Right: Sweeping arcs of silver burst from the central point of this lovely piece. Embedded white stones and tiny silver beads add glittering accents to the necklace.

DONNA LEWIS
Wristlinks
Opposite, far left: A chunky link bracelet with a rich medieval flavour. The main links are made as hollow forms for lighter wearing, while texturing and gemstones provide opulent decoration.

TIM McCREIGHT
Chopsticks
Opposite, left: These luscious pieces are made with silver metal clay and embellished with 22-carat gold and oxidation. Chopsticks make exotic hair ornaments.

BARBARA BECKER SIMON
Big Links
Opposite, below: This fabulous necklace is made with silver metal clay hollow-box forms that have been textured in a variety of ways. Stainless steel cable and sterling silver wire and hooks provide the connections.

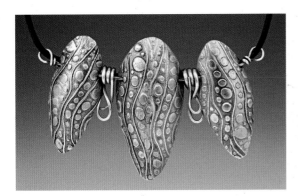

CATHERINE DAVIES PAETZ
Sea Dreams
Above: Rich colours and textures decorate the simple shapes of three hollow-form silver metal clay beads. Keum-boo and liver of sulphur embellish the surface, and silver wire and leather cord provide support.

HATTIE SANDERSON
Lidded Perfume Amphora
Right: Lovely fluid motifs decorate this small bottle with a removable lid. The silver metal clay construction is decorated with freshwater pearls and blue paua shell.

YOSHIKO SAITO

Brisk

Above & right:
The flower and leaf shapes of orchids are the inspiration for this delicate set of coordinated accessories. Stainless steel net provides support inside the silver metal clay, and the leaf veins are carved into the clay surface.

TOSHIHIDE UEEDA

Fluttering

Left: Enamel and silver leaf decorate this glorious pendant butterfly. The bold asymmetric design demonstrates the freedom that artists can achieve with metal clays.

JEANETTE LANDENWITCH
Windows to My Soul
Left: A mixture of materials has been used in this magical small wall hanging, including enamel, coloured pencil, pearl, sunstone, thread and wire.

REIKO SHO
Storage
Above: Silver paper clay combined with real pearls create an unusual brooch that has the sheen of rich satin. Folded paper techniques work beautifully in this design.

NANCY L T HAMILTON
Thistle
Right: Silver metal clay has been moulded and carved to make this classic brooch. Gemstones provide sparkle, and the lush colouring is achieved with liver of sulphur.

Templates

All templates are shown full size at 100 per cent. Simply photocopy or trace them, then use as directed in the project instructions.

PROJECT 7: INITIAL PENDANT, PAGE 50

A = Starting point for each initial
B = Second starting point for two-log initials
X = Trimming and restarting point for initials
  with pointed joins

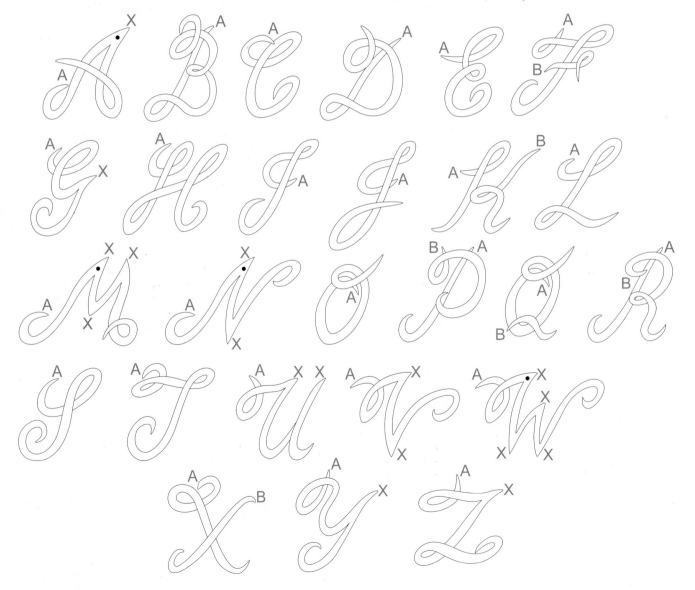

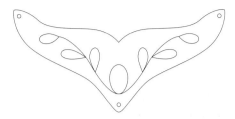

PROJECT 5: INLAID PENDANT, PAGE 46

PROJECT 6: DRAGON BROOCH, PAGE 48

PROJECT 15: CLASSIC BAND RING, PAGE 76
Adjust length as necessary.

PROJECT 20: JEWELLED FILIGREE RING, PAGE 90
Adjust length as necessary.

PROJECT 18: FEATHER EARRINGS, PAGE 86
Reverse the template when applying the filigree lines for the second earring, to make a matching pair.

PROJECT 19: LANDSCAPE PENDANT, PAGE 88

PROJECT 21: ROCK ART EARRINGS, PAGE 94
Reverse the template when cutting the clay for the second earring, to make a matching pair.

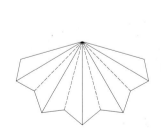

PROJECT 22: GILDED CASTLE PENDANT, PAGE 96
Cut the battlements from a separate piece of clay; the position of the battlements on the castle is indicated by dotted lines.

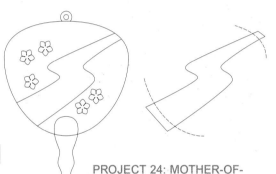

PROJECT 24: MOTHER-OF-PEARL FAN, PAGE 102
Use the template of the river on its own to mark its position on the clay, then align the river on the fan template with the dotted lines.

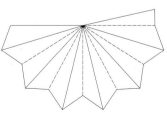

PROJECT 26: FAN EARRINGS, PAGE 112

PROJECT 26: FLOWER EARRINGS, PAGE 112

Index

Resources

Suppliers

UK
- www.thepmcstudio.com – PMC products, tools, accessories
- www.polymerclaypit.co.uk – Art Clay Silver clays, tools, findings, accessories, polymer clay, resin
- www.warm-glass.co.uk – Dichroic glass

AUSTRALIA
- www.artclaysilver.net.au – Art Clay Silver clays, polymer clays, tools, findings
- www.finnsglass.co.au – Glass-fusing tools and materials
- www.glasscoat.com.au – Glass Coat resin is a two-part resin available in Australia; see website for stockists
- www.polymerclay.com.au – PMC products, polymer clays, tools, resin

NEW ZEALAND
- www.artclaynz.co.nz – Art Clay Silver clays, tools, findings, accessories, polymer clay, resin, dichroic glass
- www.fusionglass.co.nz – PMC products, dichroic glass

USA
- www.artclayworld.com – Art Clay Silver clays, tools, findings, accessories
- www.caldroncrafts.com – Art Clay Silver clays, tools, findings, accessories
- www.coe90.com – Dichroic glass
- www.eti-usa.com/index.html – Resin
- www.nmclay.com – Art Clay Silver and PMC clays, tools, findings, accessories
- www.pmcsupply.com – PMC and Art Clay Silver clays, tools, findings, accessories
- www.wholelottawhimsy.com – Art Clay Silver and PMC clays, tools, accessories, resins, polymer clay

Guilds
There are active guilds and societies for metal clay all over the world.
UK: www.artclayworld.org.uk & www.pmcguild.co.uk
Australasia: www.artclaynz.co.nz & www.pmcguild.com.au
USA: www.artclaysociety.com & www.pmcguild.com

Hallmarking
UK: There are strict laws on selling articles that are described as precious metals unless they are hallmarked by an official Assay Office. Silver pieces under 7.78g are exempt. For more information, refer to: www.theassayoffice.co.uk/index.html
Australia: Voluntary scheme handled by the Goldsmiths and Silversmiths Guild of Australia. Refer to: www.gsga.org.au
New Zealand: No marking requirements.
Europe: Laws vary between countries. There is general information at this website with links to information in each country: en.wikipedia.org/wiki/Hallmark
USA: No marking requirements.

Credits

Picture credits

Quarto would like to thank the following artists and photographers for kindly submitting images for inclusion in the gallery.

Key: a = above, b = below, l = left, r = right

- **Akiko Adachi** (Japan) 118ar
  'At the Moment of Inheritance' – Grand Prix Award of Encouragement from the Japan Ministry of Education, Culture, Sports, Science and Technology (2006 Art Clay Silver Accessories Contest)
- **Barbara Becker Simon** 120b
  www.bbsimon.com
  photographer Larry Sanders
- **Catherine Davies Paetz** 121l
  www.cdpdesigns.com
- **Nancy L T Hamilton** 123br
  www.bellaluloo.com
- **Cindy Gard-Koizumi** 116br
  www.gardkoizumiart.com
- **Sue Heaser** 119l
  www.sueheaser.com
  photographer Phil Wilkins
- **Hadar Jacobson** 119ar
  www.artinsilver.com
- **Maki Kinoshita** (Japan) 117r
  'Beyond the River (Go for It!)' – Award from Dressmaker Gakuin (2006 Art Clay Silver Accessories Contest)
- **Mariko Konno** (Japan) 116ar
  www.lealea-m.com
  'Start' – Award from Japan Jewellery Craft School (2006 Art Clay Silver Accessories Contest)
- **Yukiko Kudo** (Japan) 117l
  home.a09.itscom.net/purete
  'Fantasy' – Grand Prix Award of Encouragement from the Japan Ministry of Education, Culture, Sports, Science and Technology (2007 Art Clay Silver Accessories Contest)

- **Jeanette Landenwitch** 123l
- **Donna Lewis** 120al
  www.donnalewis.etsy.com
- **Tim McCreight** 120ar
  www.PMCguild.com
  photographer Robert Diamante
- **Etsuko Nakayama** (Japan) 119br
  www16.plala.or.jp/silverburue/
  'Night Bloom' – Award of Encouragement from Japan Association for Leisure and Culture Development (2006 Art Clay Silver Accessories Contest)
- **Misao Oda** (Japan) 118al
  'Setsuna (The Smallest Units of Time)' – Category Award/Accessories (2006 Art Clay Silver Accessories Contest)
- **Hattie Sanderson** 121r
- **Yoshiko Saito** (Japan) 122r
  www1.vipa.ne.jp/~saitou-y
  'Brisk' – Category Award/Coordinated Accessories (2006 Art Clay Silver Accessories Contest)
- **Fumiko Sakairi** (Japan) 118b
  www.ne.jp/asahi/silver/kurepasu
  'Happy Kiss' – Award from Sygnity Japan (2006 Art Clay Silver Accessories Contest)
- **Reiko Sho** (Japan) 123ar
  'Storage' – Prejudging Candidate from the 10th Pearl Jewellery Design Contest (2006)
- **Rebecca Skeels** 116l
  www.skeels.co.uk
- **Toshihide Ueeda** (Japan) 122l 'Fluttering'
  www.ueeda.com

All other images are the copyright of Quarto Publishing plc. While every effort has been made to credit contributors, Quarto would like to apologize should there have been any omissions or errors – and would be pleased to make the appropriate correction for future editions of the book.

Author's acknowledgements

Dedication
To my husband Edward

Acknowledgments
I would like to thank the following people for their help and support:
- Seigo Mukoyama, Marc Atkinson, Daisuke Minagawa and the teaching staff of Aida Chemical Industries Co Ltd, for the Art Clay, the teaching and the encouragement.
- Lisa Cain and Tim McCreight of the PMC Guild for their help and supply of PMC for this book.
- Jean Hinton, Joan Senior and Di Tacey for keeping the Polymer Clay Pit rolling for all the months this book confined me to my studio.
- Michelle Pickering for being such an excellent editor, and Phil Wilkins for his skillful photography.
- And especially Edward, who supplied the sympathy and brought me cups of tea.